A Ru
Decisi

MW00810992

A Rulebook for Decision Making

George Pullman

Hackett Publishing Company, Inc.
Indianapolis/Cambridge

Copyright © 2015 by Hackett Publishing Company, Inc.

All rights reserved
Printed in the United States of America

18 17 16 15   1 2 3 4 5 6 7

For further information, please address
   Hackett Publishing Company, Inc.
   P.O. Box 44937
   Indianapolis, Indiana 46244-0937

   www.hackettpublishing.com

Interior and cover designs by Elizabeth L. Wilson
Composition by Aptara, Inc.

Library of Congress Cataloging-in-Publication Data

Pullman, George.
 A rulebook for decision making / George Pullman.
    pages cm
 Includes bibliographical references.
  ISBN 978-1-62466-362-8 (pbk.)—ISBN 978-1-62466-363-5 (cloth)
 1. Decision making.   2. Thought and thinking.   I. Title.
  BF448.P99 2015
  153.8′3—dc23   2014034678

The paper used in this publication meets the minimum
requirements of American National Standard for Information
Sciences—Permanence of Paper for Printed Library Materials,
ANSI Z39.48–1984.

∞

For Leola

CONTENTS

Introduction   xiii

Chapter 1: Decision Styles and Types

Decision Styles   1

Unconscious   *1*

Rule 1: Learn how to switch cruise control on and off   4

Intuitive   *4*

Rule 2: Make informed intuitive decisions   6

Rationalized   *6*

Rule 3: Avoid wishful thinking, but don't dismiss a decision merely because you made it before you were able to explain it   8

Justified   *8*

Rule 4: Don't do what you don't want to own   9

Predictive   *9*

Rule 5: Play the odds, not the game   11

Deliberate   *11*

Rule 6: Think each decision through to the beginning of the next decision   12

Summary   *12*

Rule 7: Don't let your default decision style constrain your options   13

Decision Types   14

Linked decisions   *14*

**Rule 8: Always consider the possibility that any
given decision might be linked to future decisions**   15

Indirect decisions   *15*

**Rule 9: Beware small choices that will add up
over time**   16

Threshold or tripwire decisions   *16*

**Rule 10: Make more disciplined decisions by
deciding in advance**   18

Passive decisions   *18*

**Rule 11: When accepting the default, make sure
you've thought about it and not just clicked through**   18

Delayed decisions   *18*

**Rule 12: Pay careful attention to timing, both of the
situation in which you are deciding and the situation
during which your decision will be implemented**   19

Irrevocable decisions   *19*

Rule 13: Know which bridges to burn when   21

Pseudo decisions   *21*

Rule 14: Don't waste energy on pseudo decisions   22

Stochastic versus deterministic decisions   *22*

**Rule 15: Don't apply deterministic thinking to
stochastic situations**   24

Immediate, near-term, and far-term decisions   *24*

Rule 16: You can't hit two targets with one arrow   25

Targets versus objectives   *27*

**Rule 17: For long-term goals, choose objectives
over targets**

Summary   *29*

How our brains work   *30*

**Rule 18: Don't accept System 1 solutions to
System 2 problems**   36

Rule 19: Pay attention to what you aren't thinking 38

Summary 39

Evaluating decisions 40

Rule 20: Don't think pragmatically about process-oriented decisions and vice versa 44

Summary for chapter 1 44

Chapter 2: Thinking Ahead

Foresight 46

Event horizons 47

Rule 21: Decide what to do now based on an informed opinion about what's most likely to be coming next 49

Predictive analytics 50

Rule 22: Don't just memorize the rules; ponder their implications 53

Probability 54

The probability of an event is calculated by dividing each outcome by the total number of possible outcomes (aka, the "sample space") 54

Rule 23: Don't confuse your expectations or your wishes with the actual probability of an outcome 58

Conditional probabilities 58

Rule 24: Reassess your expectations whenever new information arrives or something significant changes 60

Rule 25: The chances of two uncorrelated things happening are never greater than the change of one happening alone 61

Expected value 61

Rule 26: Expected value = outcome × probability 61

Rule 27: Don't bet against the house 62

Rule 28: Don't fall in love with an algorithm   64

Utility and marginal utility   64

**Rule 29: Don't make decisions based on false or
misleading distinctions**   65

Game Theory   66

Prisoner's dilemma   67

Maximin strategies   68

**Rule 30: Minimize your losses (and therefore the other
person's gains) as a way of maximizing your gains over time**   69

Dominant strategy   69

Rule 31: If you have a truly dominant strategy, use it   70

Ultimatum   70

**Rule 32: Do unto others as you would have
them do unto you**   71

Brinkmanship   71

**Rule 33: Don't escalate tensions unless you have
hidden reserves**   72

Truels   72

Rule 34: Don't play if you can't win   73

Dollar auction   73

Rule 35: When failure is inevitable, fail quickly and cheaply   74

Tit for tat   74

**Rule 36: Don't reward or ignore bad behavior
(your own or anyone else's)**   75

Trust   75

**Rule 37: Don't make decisions based on the
actions of unpredictable people**   76

Rule 38: Don't play at life   76

Learning to live with uncertainty   77

Alpha and beta errors   77

Rule 39: Don't confuse certainty with accuracy 79

Evidence 79

Rule 40: If you think something is true, seek
evidence to the contrary 82

Rating systems and decision making 82

Rule 41: Make certain your numbers are meaningful
and not just precise 84

Theory versus practice 85

Rule 42: Make sure your solutions are practicable 85

Overconfidence 85

Rule 43: Question twice, act once 86

Chapter 3: Decision-Making Processes

Decision-Making Processes 87

Rule 44: Develop decision-specific decision-making
processes 88

An elaborated unconscious decision process 88

The Eisenhower decision matrix 89

A simple deterministic decision process—the pros and cons list 90

Rule 45: Play the Devil's advocate 93

A model for training intuitive decision-making processes 93

An elaborated stochastic decision process 94

Rule 46: Turn your daydreams into deliberations by
focusing on every detail 99

Who are you? 100

The cognitive biases 100

Motivation 105

Rule 47: Don't provide permanent solutions to temporary
problems 107

Roles 107

The Causes of Bad Decisions   108

   Regrets   *109*

   Perspective helps   *110*

   Rule 48: Count to ten three different ways   **110**

Chapter 4: A Technique for Practicing
Your Decision-Making Skills

   Degrees of deliberative rigor   *111*

A Generalized Decision Template   113

Works Cited   115

Introduction

This primer on decisive thinking is intended for a general audience, people who have little or no familiarity with decision science, statistics, game theory, or psychology. This book is an introduction to all of these subjects with a focus on a practical approach to individual decisions. In essence, this book is about critical thinking.

While this book is called *A Rulebook for Decision Making*, don't let the title mislead you. There are no "rules" when it comes to making decisions. Life lacks the uniformity and regularity that enables anything so binding as the "laws" of physics when it comes to deciding what to do. There are, however, guidelines or heuristics, useful generalizations rather than immutable truths or indisputable conventions that can help you think more carefully about what you want and what to do before you make a decision. There are also some important ideas about how the mind works that will help you better understand your decision processes.

My goal with this book is to encourage you to think about how you think (metacognition) as a preface to making decisions. Your goal, I assume, is to make better decisions. Although this book will help you think more systematically about how you decide and give you some concrete suggestions about how to refine your decision processes, I can't promise you that refining your decision processes will necessarily lead you to better decisions. Life doesn't work that way. The best you can do is the best you can do on any given day given what you know and don't know. All the same, an informed and thoughtful decision-making process will more often than not keep the worst blunders at bay.

Everything I'm about to say about how we decide is based on the idea that each of us is a being composed of three different selves, an experiencing self, a reflective self, and a deliberate, or planning, self. Each of us tends to inhabit one of these three selves more frequently than the others and thus tends to make decisions primarily consistent with that self. The experiential self lives in the present moment, focused on fulfilling immediate needs and desires and dealing with anxieties, frustrations, and pleasures. It has no sense of time, neither that things will change nor that they have been other than they currently are. The reflective self has a meta-perspective on life and is inclined to ponder how things got the way they are. It focuses on the past, searching for patterns and explanations that might help make sense of the present or offer advice about what to do in order to achieve a specific future. The deliberate self is the planning, organizing, visionary self. It readily imagines possible futures and seeks either to realize or avoid depending on what it predicts.

Each of the three selves influences how you make decisions. The experiential self is impulsive but also, when properly trained, intuitive, that is, it seeks to solve problems without conscious thought in advance of or reflection after a decision. The reflective self looks back over past events to see if there's something in the thought process or the unfolding of events that may explain how things got the way they did. It seeks to improve outcomes through thinking about previous decisions, and in this way it might be said to raise the unconscious to consciousness. The planning self is calculating (in a good way), predictive, and conscious about what it is doing and why. This book will help you understand how we move among the selves and give you some techniques for priming the reflective self in order to cultivate the planning self. At the same time, however, I'm not privileging the planning self or even the reflective self over the experiencing self, as books on decision science typically do. Some decision situations are better suited to the experiencing self, others to the deliberate self. Sometimes you need to get out of your head, as the sports psychologists say, turn off the reflective mind and let the unconscious take over. Other times you will need to stop and ask yourself why you are doing what you are doing in order to find a way out of a counterproductive routine. And of course there will be opportunities in life that are much more likely realized by careful planning. While such moments may seem the most important, it's often the lesser, habit-forming decisions, like choosing to drink soda or watch TV in the evening, that may have the greatest impact on your life. When it comes to deciding, no one process and no one self is necessarily best. You have to learn about how you think before you can think at your best.

Before we get to all of that, however, take a few minutes to reflect on your default decision-making self.

Your Turn

1. If the number 100 represents your full self, what percentage of the time in a given day do you spend inhabiting each self?

Reflective		Experiential		Deliberate	

2. How can you verify your estimation?

3. Can you think of a decision you made a few months or even a year or so ago that you would make differently now? If so, what changed?

4. What was the last decision you made that you thought deeply about before you made it?

5. Do you consider yourself a spontaneous person?

CHAPTER 1
Decision Styles and Types

Decision Styles

We don't all think alike, of course, but each of us also thinks differently in different contexts. We tend to be more impatient when we are hungry, for example, when our experiential self asserts itself because an important need needs immediate attention. When our immediate needs are taken care of and we need to make a decision similar to one we've made in the past, we might find our reflective self stepping up. If the decision situation seems to be novel, we might find the deliberate self taking over. Each of the selves has a different decision style: unconscious, semiconscious or intuitive, and fully conscious or deliberate. Because each of us tends to inhabit one self more often than the others, each of us has a default decision style. Some of us tend toward intuition, for example, while others like to calculate the odds of an outcome and work out the details in detail before deciding. I am of course oversimplifying, but simple is sometimes a good way to begin. Let's look at the major decision styles.

Unconscious

Unconscious decisions are the result of unobserved mental processes that manifest themselves as preferences, inclinations, or tendencies. We make hundreds of unconscious decisions every day: get up early or sleep in; exercise now, later, or not at all; tee shirt 'n' jeans or power suit; car, public transit, or bike; skip lunch, eat lunch on the job, or go out; Thai or burgers[1]; throw a few coins in a street musician's case or walk by unmoved; Chrome, Firefox, Explorer, or Safari? Our days are

---

1. According to food psychologist Brian Wansink, we make 200 decisions daily just about what to eat (Kindle Locations 2006, 82–83).

filled with moments when we might consciously choose one alternative over others but don't because it doesn't occur to us to think about it; so unconscious are we in fact that we might not even notice options exist. We are following routines that are a consequence of conscious or semiconscious decisions we made so long ago we don't remember making them (habits) or following behavioral patterns we inherited from our parents or learned unconsciously from the people we grew up with or with whom we work and live that silently and instantly, as it were, advise us what to do. You can think of these decision routines as scripts in the sense of brief computer programs written to accomplish specific tasks as quickly and efficiently as possible—rather than deciding every night when to get up the next morning, just get up every morning at the same time.

While you are probably willing to agree that many of your daily choices are made with little or no conscious thought, would you also be willing to agree that your life-altering decisions are made in the same way? Do you now or have you ever questioned your religious faith, for example? What about your decision to marry, have children, go to college, or work? What about your career path? Has that been a sequence of planned moves based on analysis of the situation, a set of somewhat random opportunities, or a chance encounter followed by a kind of cruise control existence?

Many people know what they believe and how they want to live without consciously thinking through all of the possible alternatives or even comparing and contrasting the most obvious ones, to say nothing of pondering the possible alternative outcomes of their choices as a way of thinking about what to do. Opportunities arise unannounced and unbidden while others disappear as if at random (sometimes truly randomly), and we simply react to the stimuli that present themselves based on our unexamined inclinations and assumptions, our preference routines.

If you are disinclined to consciously examine your options and content to be the person you currently find yourself to be, living primarily in the experiencing self, reacting to opportunities, challenges, and experiences as they present themselves and otherwise swimming with the current, or if you believe that life is uncontrollably random and therefore that planning and calculation are delusional, then your decision style is unconscious, a form of fatalism. The world just is the way it is. What happens to me is what will be and I just have to make the best of it (or rail against it, but it won't matter either way). There are many variations of fatalism, from the metaphysical (fate), to the ludic (luck), to the biological (genes are destiny), to the socio-logical (poverty thinking, affluenza). But they are all premised on the ultimate tautology: it is what it is. You don't make decisions, not con-sciously anyway. Things just happen, and you just are. You spend most of your time in the experiencing self.

There's nothing inherently wrong with a fatalistic decision-making style. Many people live perfectly happy and productive lives by select-ing the defaults in every situation, living permanently in the present focused on experiences and accepting opportunities and challenges as they come. Even people who see themselves primarily as deliber-ate thinkers, planners, may accept a wide range of defaults so they can concentrate their energy on more important decisions. Ten min-utes debating the costs and benefits of Thai over Mexican food for lunch today is ten minutes that could be spent texting or reading a chapter in a book about decision making. Giving decisions over to the unconscious, living on cruise control, frees up consciousness. But the downside—there's always a downside—of living on cruise con-trol is routinization. If you never consciously decide anything, you lack awareness of the processes that lead you to become the person you are. Worse, your lack of practice at conscious deciding may make it harder to think through your options, or even see that you have any, when something out of the ordinary happens. If nothing else, an inveterate commitment to fatalism makes reading a book like this kind of pointless.

Unconscious decisions are not expressed in words, but if they were, they would sound something like, "I want X: Zoink!" Unconscious decision processes have a powerful effect on our daily lives because they are our habits of mind. Given a specific input, we always produce the same output. Anxiety becomes "I'm hungry." A feeling of achieve-ment becomes "Let's party." The need for acceptance and belonging becomes "Go Team." If you want to break a mental habit, you can rewrite a decision script or at least turn cruise control off momen-tarily by asking not "*What* do I want?" but rather "*Why* do I want that?" (Much easier said than done, of course.) At the same time, if you want to become extremely efficient at any task, mental or physical, repeat-ing the task over and over can embed it in the unconscious and thus make it instantly available. Anything that requires thought takes at least a moment to happen. Zoink! Is fast and fast can be very useful in some decision settings. But of course fast can be disastrous when something other than routine thought is required. What is bad some-times is sometimes good.

Rule 1: Learn how to switch cruise control on and off

Your Turn

1. Make a list of your habitual behaviors. Can you track down the decisive moment that led to each preference or inclination? Did you inherit each habit from a parent or absorb it from a friend?

2. See if you can identify a habit of mind, a decision you always find yourself making whenever you find yourself in that situation. How did you come by that habit of mind and what are some alternatives that don't occur to you normally?

3. Look up the *Einstellung effect*. Can you think of a decision you made that was based entirely on a previous decision? The first four cars I owned were Honda Accords. Lovely, dependable cars those. Don't fix what ain't broke? Or lack of imagination? Brand loyalty? Or routinization?

Intuitive

There are decision situations when you quickly zero in on what seems like the best possible option, simulate or visualize what will happen in your head, and then go with the plan confident that you've made the right decision. We often call these gut-level, instinctive, or intuitive decisions, in which after a brief pause (a moment of indecision) we arrive at what we are sure is the right thing to do. We don't stop to explain the choice or question the evidence we used to arrive at it. We just "know" that this person is trustworthy and that shirt matches these pants and this ball is going over that fence. We don't have a fully worked out theory; we just know.

Intuitive decisions are fast and when based on deep experience they can be very effective as well. When based on unwarranted or unexamined assumptions, however, they can lead to unfortunate consequences of the "What-was-I-thinking?" variety. Up until recently intuition has gotten little respect in the decision-making literature.

Gary Klein and his colleagues have done a great deal to remedy this situation under the heading of what they call "naturalistic" decision making. We will revisit the idea of trained intuition later. If you are really interested, you should read Klein's *Sources of Power* (1999). You might also find Gerd Gigerenzer's talk *Simple Heuristics That Make Us Work* (2001) interesting. There's also Malcolm Gladwell's *Blink: The Power of Thinking without Thinking* (2005).

If you make most of your decisions in a semi-conscious and quasi-analytical, sketch-on-the-back-of-the-napkin kind of way then your decision style is intuitive. Intuition is reliable when disciplined by broad and deep experience and limited to spheres directly touching that experience. Absent that deep learning, an intuitive style can be prejudicial, reactionary, or merely conventional (default decisions). Intuitive decisions can be fast and effective when cultural norms and expectations, the unexamined assumptions from which the decision to act is inferred, are aligned with the circumstances in which you have to decide. Even if the data and the way you are inclined to interpret them are misaligned, the difference may never matter to you if you fail to notice the discrepancy, for example, or choose to ignore the evidence. On the other hand, if an intuitive decision leads to unfortunate or unintended consequences, you're left just basically astonished, with no process to reflect on and refine and no ready justification if any one questions you.

In essence, an intuitive decision can be expressed as, "I want X but I can't get it directly. I need, hmm, what do I need? Q looks and feels right. Q then." When deciding intuitively, many of the steps are left unsaid and in some cases even unthought. We just hopscotch from spot to spot in order to get where we think we want to be, without pondering the value of the goal or its potential unintended consequences or our motivations for pursuing that goal in the first place. If this, then that: go.

There's a slightly more analytical variation of an intuitive decision style: "I want an X. What are the features that I want in an X? It has to have B, C, D, and not R." Then one simply measures the candidates against the feature list and whichever one has the most matches gets the nod, unless there are no good candidates or something in the matching process alters our criteria. If after sorting through several candidates you wind up with more than one that meets your criteria, you can flip a coin to see if they really balance (if it lands heads and you are suddenly inclined to toss the coin again, you know the balance wasn't real). If the viable candidates don't balance, compare the absent features, what each lacks, the downsides (subsequent costs, for example). If one candidate has absolutely everything you are looking for except the one thing you need more than anything else, they are probably a bad candidate, though abandoning them in anticipation of disappointment may prove more difficult than choosing them and then dealing with the inevitable disappointment at a later time. Some insights are best learned through experience.

Intuitive deciders tend to spend most of their time in their experiencing self.

Once we start pondering our goals as well as the alternative methods for achieving them, we're moving away from intuition toward more overtly conscious forms of deciding. Overt consciousness isn't always preferable. Sometimes decisions have to be made quickly, and at such times, intuition is best, especially if it has experience behind it.

Rule 2: Make informed intuitive decisions

Rationalized

Rationalization is a process of explaining a decision after it has been made. Once you've done something or decided to do it, you may feel compelled to explain your choice. Although we tend to use the word "rationalization" in a negative way, as in the idea of explaining away a bad decision or excusing ourselves for the questionable thing we're about to do, there is a more positive usage. When we make an intuitive decision, one based entirely on rapid inference from experience (or prejudice[2]) and without conscious forethought, we may feel

---

2. The word "prejudice" has a universally bad connotation, but it really just means a pre-judgment and its negative connotation says more about the dominance of analytical decision-making practices than the nature of the idea. Sure, stereotypes are thoughtless and assumptions about common things can be greatly misleading, but it also sometimes happens that our reflexive interpretations of events and people have merit. Life is more complex than our impatient minds would like. There was a great example of the problem inherent in pre-judgment in Texas about the time I was writing this section. You may recall it. A girl was traveling to a dance competition with her adult male dance partner and their adult male coach. The coach had papers signed

compelled to "show our work" to ourselves. Just because we decided first and then explained ourselves later doesn't mean we've behaved irrationally. For a rationalization to be successful it has to connect motivation to decision in a plausible way. If the explanation seems like an excuse or just wishful thinking, the rationalization becomes a *mere* rationalization. It also sometimes happens that the connection between the decision and the explanation is so farfetched that it warrants the label "confabulation" rather than "explanation." You need to learn how to distinguish a sound explanation from an excuse and an excuse from wishful or fabulous thinking, to say nothing of blatant hypocrisy. (You also need to develop a sense of humor about the mistakes you will make standing by an outrageous explanation from time to time because we all do it; it's part of learning, of growing up but also of growing old.) Just because you can't explain why you decided to do something doesn't mean it was an irrational decision. It may just be that you don't quite know how to articulate your intuition, and in such cases you're better off not rationalizing because you might be deluding yourself in the process.

Rationalizers tend to live primarily in their reflective self.

If you rationalize your decisions in front of others, you leave yourself open to second-guessing. Unless you are making a collective decision, you shouldn't rationalize in public.

If you like to decide intuitively and explain your decisions after you've made them, in order to understand yourself better through reflection or to refine your decision-making practices, you have a rationalized decision style. As long as you really are explaining why you prefer one thing to another and not just making stuff up to protect yourself from self-criticism or hide hypocrisy or some ill-fated impulse, rationalizing can be a useful way to train your intuitions.

---

by the girl's mother authorizing the trip. Both adult males were black and the girl was white. As they were catching a few hours of sleep late at night in a gas station, a police officer looked in the car and saw a girl with two apparently unrelated men. He arrested them and they weren't released until after the paper work was verified. To many observers the authorities behaved in a typically racist fashion. But you could just as easily argue that such an interpretation is an egregious application of the stereotype "Texan law enforcement," that the authorities were merely following procedure closely in a case where the skin colors facilitated a pre-judgment against them. If the authorities wanted to contain the obvious impending controversy, they should have moved much faster to figure out what the actual situation was or taken the suspects at their word, but that would have taken some seriously independent thinking (Edwards 2013).

If, on the other hand, you really don't know what you are doing and get good at making up excuses, you will have perfected delusional thinking.

Rule 3: Avoid wishful thinking, but don't dismiss a decision merely because you made it before you were able to explain it

Justified

Justification is a process of defending a decision against accusations of irrationality or insensitivity or unethical, abnormal, inappropriate, or even just foolish behavior. Like rationalization, justification is retrospective, backward looking. Unlike rationalization, justification is typically a public act. Having said that, however, it is worth pointing out that one form of decision making is to imagine how you will justify a decision once your actions become public knowledge. This isn't just about how it's easier to get forgiveness than permission; it's about shining the light of public scrutiny on yourself and projecting yourself into the future as a way of evaluating your plans through other people's eyes. You may decide that you don't care how others see what you are planning to do or that you do and they will approve, or you may think twice about doing it, having pondered how you will justify it. This kind of dissociative thinking, in which you create a distinction between your present and future self and your personal experience and the public perception of yourself, is very difficult to learn how to do. Many of us live egocentrically in the ever present, focused on what we want right now and only vaguely aware of what is going to happen as a consequence later on or how others might perceive what we are doing. This is why long-term behavioral change is so hard, why we eat mindlessly, for example, and fail to exercise routinely or save money or study when there's no test coming. Self-justification may be unpleasant, but it's healthy if done properly. If done improperly, self-justification becomes self-righteousness or the public equivalent of wishful thinking.

Justifiers live primarily between their reflective and their planning self.

If you make a point of explaining yourself to yourself before you make a decision, if you don't like to do anything that you can't justify in advance, then you have a justificatory decision style. Even if the thought of justifying a decision before you make it has never occurred to you before, you might find the exercise useful. If you ever plan to do something radical, something that will definitely garner close questioning, being practiced at the arts of justification will come in handy. If, on the other hand, you feel oppressed by the idea that you might need to justify your actions, you might want to think about whether you are refusing servitude (or accountability) or just refusing to squarely confront your motivations or lack of self-reflection.

Rule 4: Don't do what you don't want to own

Predictive

Predictive decision making is a process of deciding what to do based on expectations about what is going to happen in the future. How you derive that future tells you a great deal about how you think.

Scientific thinking is a particularly rigorous form of predictive thinking. "Given a model of how B works (a hypothesis), if variable R is held constant while electricity is applied, it is predicted Z will increase by a factor of one." You don't need to be a scientist working in a laboratory to make decisions this way. Whenever you have a model of how something works and imagine a future state based on that model undergoing some process (even if that process is just time), you are using predictive thinking. If you modify your model based on the results of your interventions, you are adding reflection into the thought process and thinking in a highly analytical and systematic way.

If you prefer to make decisions in tightly controlled environments, where everything relevant is clearly on the table and the consequence of each action is predictable, then you have an analytical decision-making style. You don't like surprises and you don't like mistakes. The downside of an analytical decision style is not all decision situations can be scientifically controlled. In such cases, the analytically inclined have to adopt a more intuitive style or they may artificially or unconsciously eliminate the ambiguity and complexity in the situation, creating a false solution or a careless decision. For analytical thinkers who can't switch to more intuitive forms of thinking, the best option is to limit their decisions to situations that can be tightly controlled, the laboratory, the clean room, or wherever everything relevant can be identified and coordinated.

Diagnostic thinking is scientific thinking in reverse. You try to figure out why something is the way it is. Create a theory about how it got that way. Change something. Assess the result. Rethink your theory. Try it again. If you are systematic and change only one variable at a time, eventually you may zero in on the source of the problem and if you are working in a fairly deterministic setting, like trying to get a piece of computer code to work or figure out why a fan isn't working, then by this thought process you can fix problems. We call this kind of thinking "troubleshooting." While you can't troubleshoot the future, you can decide what to do based on an understanding of how a process works, anticipating where it will eventually break down, and so decide to reinforce that spot or stockpile resources for dealing with the inevitable breakdown.

If you like to look at decision situations as problems to be solved, then you have a troubleshooter's style.

Another form of predictive thinking, more like mathematics than science, is probabilistic thinking. Here you are simply asking what the chances of an outcome are and deciding what to do on the basis of those chances. People are not especially good at probabilistic reasoning for reasons we will look at in the section on thinking ahead. But learning to think probabilistically is very important. If nothing else, you should learn to appreciate the linguistic fact that *risk* does not approximate *threat*. Risk taking is an important part of thoughtful and informed decision making.

In essence, a predictive decision looks something like this: "Given this set of conditions, I predict X will happen next; therefore, I'm going to do Y."

If you enjoy deciding on the basis of prediction, and you aren't thinking in the controlled environment of a laboratory, then you have a gambler's decision style, an eye for odds and quite likely a desire to be proven right in time. Having a gambler's style isn't the same thing as being reckless. People who put a million dollars on red 15 aren't gambling because the odds are not in their favor. They are spending their money on the dopamine-infused thrill experienced in the fractional second before the ball drops. That's not gambling. Gamblers don't make improbable bets. They know the odds and they are willing to play them. Losing is factored into the bottom line. Some decisions are risky. Knowing how to calculate the odds of an outcome and so decide what risks to take is an important life skill.

Predictive deciders tend to live primarily in their planning self.

Rule 5: Play the odds, not the game

Deliberate

Deliberation is a fully conscious, overtly analytical, prediction-based process of deciding among all plausible options using all of the available data and reflecting on the importance of missing or dubious data. Often the word "deliberation" is reserved for group decision making, especially with reference to a jury. But whenever a group of people with common or related interests gets together to choose a course of action that will benefit them all if it succeeds and harm them all if it fails, however abstractly or even unequally, you have a deliberative decision situation. Whenever you talk to yourself in a similar way, thinking about the pros and cons, calculating the probabilities, estimating the rewards, weighing the risks, preparing for possible contingencies and unintended consequences, and so on as you plan a course of action with some near but mostly long-term payoffs, you are deliberating with yourself. The more intentional, reflective, computational, and self-aware your decision in favor of one course of action over another is, the more deliberate you are being.

If you like to ponder the long-term consequences of various options in advance of choosing, focusing primarily on evidence and implications, probabilities and potentials, then your decision style is deliberate. A lot of the textbooks on decision making focus on deliberation to the exclusion of the other styles, partially because it seems the most "rational," and partially because it can be taught. Intuition has to be learned and the difference between taught and learned is the difference between a course and a career. For many reasons that we will explore as we go along, "rational" decision making is an over-simplification of how real decisions, even deliberate ones, get made. Moreover, not all decisions will admit of a deliberate process. Some common conditions that disable deliberation are when the evidence is scanty or the time is short or your goals are indistinct to you. But there will also be times when you might make a better decision if you worked out all the details in greater detail and impatience alone or inexperience led you to choose a quicker, less deliberate process.

At any rate, the essence of a deliberate decision process might be expressed like this: "I think I want to spend the next several years pursuing X. Why? And why do I want that? And why? OK, what I really want is RX. So how do I get RX? There are three approaches. Approach 1 has these steps each with these chances, risks, constraints, and costs. Approach 2 has these steps each with these chances, risks, constraints, and costs. Approach 3 has these steps, these constraints and costs, and these chances of success. Therefore, I will go with 2 and prepare for modifications as I go."

Planners live almost exclusively in their planning self, spending perhaps some time reflecting and, like everyone, sometimes experiencing without conscious thought, but for the most part they are looking ahead and trying to figure out the best way to get where they want to be next.

Rule 6: Think each decision through to the beginning of the next decision

Summary

The most important take away from this section on the decision styles is that your default decision style is not your only option. You can harness your impulses, instruct your intuition, and learn how to calculate probabilities. You can also choose a style based on your interpretation of the nature of the decision you are facing. Don't limit your cognitive options based on unexamined assumptions about who you are. You can learn, and therefore you can change. If you don't inhabit your planning self very often and prefer in fact to live almost entirely in the present moment, that's fine, but that is no reason to refuse to learn how to calculate probabilities. Similarly, even if you live in your planning self more often than you do your immediate self, you should think about how to train your intuitions in order to make accurate decisions more quickly.

You should also keep in mind that what you do for a living will likely alter which self you tend to inhabit. If you are in logistics, for example, you will spend your day planning. If you are a writer in any sense of the word, you will spend your days deep in your reflective self. There is something called "occupational psychosis," in which all facets of your life are assimilated into the way you make a living. This may or may not be a bad state of cognitive affairs, but the healthiest way to live might be to seek a balanced self, sometimes experiencing, sometimes reflecting, and sometimes planning.

Rule 7: Don't let your default decision style constrain your options

Your Turn

1. What is your default decision style?
   - Unconscious, fatalistic
   - Semiconscious, intuitive
   - Rationalized
   - Justified
   - Predictive, scientific, probabilistic
   - Deliberate

2. How well did your self-analysis from the first section match your default decision style?

3. If you have different styles in different settings, what kind of setting goes with which style?

Decision Types

Now that you are aware of your default decision style and have a sense of how your default might be preferable in some situations and less preferable in others, let's look at some of the different kinds of decisions you face.

Linked decisions

Linked decisions are exactly what the phrase suggests, a decision that is connected to another one. Sometimes there are multiple, interrelated connections. Linked decision making is strategic or logistical thinking. It is the purview of the planning self when focused on the future, but sometimes you will be wondering how the current options came to be what they are, a kind of how-did-I-get-here? moment, and at such times the reflective self will be online.

Game theorists, about which more later, have a puzzle called the traveling salesperson problem. It's a logistics optimization problem useful for determining delivery routes and other point-by-point paths (like in a circuit board). The basic problem is what is the most efficient way for a person to travel from place to place stopping at each one only once? Imagine you are hand delivering holiday presents. You've got five friends all over town. What order do you give the presents in? Obviously the question gets answered differently if the only consideration is the shortest route. Take traffic patterns and the various schedules of your friends into account, and the problem becomes more complicated. As always, everything hinges on the definition of the key terms and, in this case, what does "efficiency" mean? Maybe you should just host a party.

The traveling salesperson puzzle is an interesting metaphor for planning that requires designing efficient patterns and accounting for numerous variables. From this perspective it's an interesting way to practice linked decision making. Each node represents the outcome of a decision from which one has then to make another and then from the next spot another, always taking into account the ultimate goal and various values maintained along the way (save gas and time in the salesperson example), but those values would change as the paradigm morphs into other experiences (like navigating a college curriculum or planning a career or raising a child). The advantage of using the traveling salesman as a decision-making paradigm is that it offers a more systematic approach to deciding by linking decisions together for a single purpose. Logistics is a decision-making practice based on a given and therefore unquestioned or at least no longer questioned goal, with the result that it is focused entirely on *how* questions and indifferent to *why* questions.

If a decision is linked to others, each decision influences the next one. If it's possible to see a goal as the result of a series of decisions, it may be possible to gain some advantage by linking the decisions up. If two decisions are in conflict, then you have a prior decision to make about values and goals.

Positionality—figuring out where you need to be based on where you currently are and where you hope to be in the future—is an important version of linked decision making. Before you decide to move in a particular direction, given a sense of the range of options from which you are going to choose in the future, it might make a great deal of sense to start assembling your resources, developing the skills you will need, cultivating the relationships that will be important, saving your money, preserving your energy, and so on.

If you like planning, then linking decisions appeals to you. You like itineraries and structured to do lists and schedules and charts. You like to plan and forecast. You probably get kind of nervous when you can't see the next stone on the path. And you might even prefer a known outcome to a better but doubtful one. If you don't like logistics, if you prefer to think of each decision as a discrete moment, being influenced by nothing that preceded it and having no influence over subsequent decisions, then you are a hard core intuitionist, but you may also need to broaden your horizons.

Rule 8: Always consider the possibility that any given decision might be linked to future decisions

Indirect decisions

Sometimes we make decisions about one thing while thinking about something else. Often this happens while inhabiting the experiencing self, as we are focused on the sensations of the present moment and not reflecting on the possible consequences or thinking about how the present links to the future. Remember, the experiencing self has no sense of the future.

The people you meet are a function of the place where you live, for example. If you love food, to take another example, or use it as a way to soothe life's frustrations and struggles or celebrate its happy moments, you might end up with weight issues and, more than likely, the attendant health problems. If just before the last time you had a stomach virus you were eating chestnuts, you might decide to never eat chestnuts again or even, if you have an active imagination, that you are allergic to them. Creating a general principle based on an immediate and vivid experience can create a habit of mind, resulting in future decision moments that you will handle as a selection moment rather than a decision moment. In other words, sometimes once we decide, all subsequent decisions of that type are made automatically from then on. The butterfly effect, while ponderable on a cosmic level, is real for each of us in the sense that what we do now will influence what we do and even can and can't do later.

Let's take a mundane example. How much does a large coffee cost in your neighborhood? And how about something for the coffee to wash down? You have to eat breakfast, right? Let's say you do that three times a week. Over a year, what does that cost? From an experiential perspective it's just a bagel and a cup of coffee, your morning routine, a comforting situation-normal kind of regular experience. From a planning perspective it's what, 15 dollars a week, 780 dollars a year? Since we just became more conscious of the decision we were making, we might also want to recognize that bagels are around 400 calories each.

Our days are filled with drops in a bucket, small, apparently insignificant choices that over time create the pails of water we carry.

Rule 9: Beware small choices that will add up over time

Threshold or tripwire decisions

There's also a class of predictive thinking that we might call "threshold" or "tripwire" deciding. Sometimes it's a good idea to make a decision in advance in order to restrain your experiencing self from making an impulsive decision in the heat of a moment or to keep your experiencing self from letting a situation get out of hand. Remember, the experiencing self doesn't think ahead. So, for example, you might decide that you will end a relationship the very first time a person lies to you. Were you to break this rule, you might find yourself in a situation later that would be much harder to correct, saddled with children, a mortgage, and a cheating spouse, for example.

There are less depressing applications of tripwire decisions as well. You might decide, for example, to sell a stock when it gets to a certain level or a house when it hits a specific value. If you put off deciding until the moment to get out has arrived, you risk getting swept away by enthusiasm and then dropped painfully back to earth when the bubble bursts. You may also suffer from what is called the sunk-cost fallacy, in which you keep spending money on a lost cause because you can't bear to give up on it. You've come so far; you're so close. The longer you focus on "so close" the more money and time you are losing. If you draw the line before the process starts, it will be easier to get out if it all goes bad. Never enter anything without an exit strategy.

Threshold decisions are also a way of trying to prevent the cognitive bias known as the "normalcy effect." When people are in a crisis they sometimes fail to react. At the far negative end of the spectrum you have people sitting like statues, seat-belted down as the cabin fills with smoke and the emergency exit doors are thrown open. Panic has set in and they are paralyzed. A much less extreme case sometimes happens when a clearly forecast disaster unfolds so slowly that people don't bother to heed the warning. I've seen this happen in Atlanta in the winter, where it snows every couple of years and there's little in the way of snow-removal equipment or mass transit. Snow is forecast and nearly everyone thinks, "Two inches. No big deal." And instead of going home they go have a nice lunch or hang around talking with friends, in anticipation of getting a snow day tomorrow. Soon there's an inch of snow covering a thin layer of ice on the highways and everyone leaves for home at once. But there's no snow-removal equipment and no one has snow tires; the highways quickly clog up with fender benders and then here and there a truck jackknifes, and within an hour or so what was a ninety-minute commute has become an overnighter on the side of the road in your car. The danger was clearly forecast and the remedy was obvious, and yet people let it happen because the life-as-normal decision-making process is so hard to circumvent. For more on the normalcy bias, see *You Are Not So Smart* (McRaney 2012).

There's a variation of the threshold decision that goes by the acronym IFTTT: if this, then that. It's a software trigger, essentially. When something happens, you ask the software you are using to do something, not just send a notification, but do something in particular. So, for example, if you arrive at the mall, send a coupon for your favorite store. If it's Valentine's Day, send your significant other a digital card. If Apple hits 600, sell, and so on.

Rule 10: Make more disciplined decisions by deciding in advance

Passive decisions

Some decisions are passive, in which you choose the default, either joining the group or following the leader or following a trend, acquiescence essentially. If you just find yourself going with the crowd, unaware of the moment when your feet left the ground, then at that moment you are living inside your experiencing self exclusively. On the other hand, if you actually said to yourself, "I'm going with the default here," then you let your reflective self break in for a moment, to accept consciously a decision made by somebody else or by circumstances beyond any one person's control. Such decisions are not exactly unconscious, but they are still passive because all you decided was to accept.

Rule 11: When accepting the default, make sure you've thought about it and not just clicked through

Delayed decisions

Choosing to delay a decision is a decision. While we tend to think of procrastination as counterproductive, it might be the best decision if further information is required or circumstances might change in the foreseeable future. Waiting is sometimes known as the "Fabian Strategy," after the Roman general who advocated delaying a direct confrontation with Hannibal, who was pillaging and plundering the Roman territories. Many Romans accused Fabian of cowardice for advocating delay. When the hawks finally won the debate, they immediately sent the soldiers to confront Hannibal wherever they found him. They found him at Cannae and charged onto the field of battle before they realized the battlefield was bottle shaped. They were instantly surrounded and quickly annihilated—the worst Roman military defeat ever. Had they waited until Hannibal occupied a less disadvantageous space, they might have fared much better. But waiting would have meant watching more compatriots fall to the invader and more crops consumed by their enemies while they and their friends suffered outrageously. Resisting the impulse to react is often a difficult decision to make. To make such moments even harder, it is also possible to wait too long.

So if you feel as though you need to do something in particular but you find yourself putting it off, rather than upbraiding yourself for being lazy or cowardly, first consider whether or not there might be a good reason for waiting. Perhaps you're thinking something through, or waiting for something relevant to happen, or waiting to see what someone else does or what happens next. Maybe you need to finish something already underway. You may have a good reason to wait, in other words. And then again, maybe you are just delaying so that there won't be enough time to really challenge yourself, so you can protect yourself from the harsher self-assessment that comes from having tried hard but failed anyway.

Rule 12: Pay careful attention to timing, both of the situation in which you are deciding and the situation during which your decision will be implemented

Irrevocable decisions

Some decisions have unalterable consequences. Once such a decision is made, everything changes and there's no control-alt-delete. When you recognize a decision as irrevocable, you may feel paralyzed by the enormity of the situation or you may feel like procrastinating even though you know you shouldn't. You might find yourself waffling. Should I stay or should I go? It also sometimes happens that you can't make up your mind because you aren't fully committed. In such cases, forcing a commitment *might* be a good decision to make.

There's a fairly common piece of advice never to burn your bridges. Typically this advice is offered as a restraint against an impulse to hurt someone's feelings or cause a stink out of anger or frustration. If you insult an employer on the way out the door, you won't get a letter of reference, obviously, but you might also get a reputation for being a prima donna or a jerk, and most worlds are much smaller than they look. Don't step over people on your way up because you never know whom you will meet on the way down. And so on. You don't even need to believe in Karma to appreciate this.

The expression, however, "to burn one's bridges" actually had a different meaning when it first entered the world of ideas during the warring states period in China. The advice is this: if you need your troops to fight the enemy on the other side of a river, then you need to build a bridge across the river. Once your soldiers have crossed the bridge, they can't retreat if you burn the bridge. Your soldiers will have to accept only one set of options: death or glory. In other words, to force a decision, burn your bridges.

At the same time, if you leave your enemies no egress, they too will be forced to fight to the death. So while you might want to burn your own bridges, don't burn theirs unless you have superior resources (or are prepared to die fighting). Do anything you can to increase your resolve without increasing your opposition's resolve if you are facing a competitive decision situation.

In a non-military context, leaving an out, keeping your options open, is a good idea when there are many options to choose from or when nothing in particular stands out as preferable, or when the situation is dynamic and new information may arrive shortly and change everything. But sometimes you will need to commit yourself fully to a single course of action in order to accomplish anything at all, and in those situations knowing where the exits are may weaken your resolve. If you find yourself waffling out of fear or uncertainty but know at some deeper level that what you are feeling is just anxiety and not doubt, then commit irrevocably: burn your bridges.

One simple way to burn a bridge is to tell other people of your intentions. You are much more likely to do something if you tell people you intend to. Saying we will do something and then not following through creates cognitive dissonance in most people, thus pledging works. Car dealers sometimes use this technique. If I can get you the price you want will you buy the car? OK, will you sign this nonbinding agreement to that effect? Same deal. It's important to realize that if you make others feel like they have no choice, they will comply if they are essentially passive people, but if they are more aggressive, they may well lie or cheat to get what they want.

You may want to keep in mind the fact that there are always two bridges to burn, the one that leads forward and the one that leads back. In other words, whenever you think about committing to a course of action you should at least consider committing to its opposite. The moment *before* you cross the bridge you just built you should ask yourself, do I burn this now, do I burn it once I've crossed it, or do I leave it up and open so I can commute?

Rule 13: Know which bridges to burn when

Pseudo decisions

There is a category of decisions we might call "pseudo" or "fake" decisions in which you seem to have alternatives but they don't amount to real alternatives for one of several reasons. They may all be basically the same. With no differences that matter, there's no real decision to make. This is why branding is so important in consumer societies. It creates apparent differences where no actual differences exist. In pseudo decision cases in which the options are all basically the same, they may all be equally undesirable (we call these "dilemmas"), or they may all be equally good (we call these "toss-ups"). Another pseudo decision involves one alternative that is so vastly superior to the others that comparison is useless. There are also some pseudo decisions created by the fact that the various options are so completely different from each other that there's no basis of comparison and therefore no way to establish a comparative preference (apples to oranges). In such decision situations, unless you can find a common denominator, just flip a coin. Finally, we often ponder what we should do in case something really bad happens. This is sometimes called "borrowing trouble" and it is generally a waste of energy and a source of pointless anxiety. Most of the things we worry about don't happen to us. That's not cancer. The plane isn't crashing. Your kid doesn't hate you. Thinking about the worst case scenario is a waste of time if the worst case is, as it often is, irrelevant.

All pseudo decision situations require arbitrary decisions. You could just flip a coin or cast a die or even just walk away. If a decision really doesn't matter to you because you are sure it's a pseudo decision, you could let someone else decide. However, if you make a habit of off-loading pseudo decisions on to others, you may come across as passive or indecisive and that may have an unintended effect on your relationships. Sometimes making what seems to you like a purely arbitrary decision might help you avoid making an indirect decision. You should also keep in mind that because some decisions have unintended consequences, an arbitrary decision might lead to a significant one.

Rule 14: Don't waste energy on pseudo decisions

Stochastic versus deterministic decisions

The list of decision types I've just given you is by no means complete, but it is probably more than enough to get you thinking about how thinking needs to happen in a context, how knowing what kind of decision you are making can help you make better decisions or at least restrain you from making hasty ones. We could extend the list. In fact, you should see if you can add to it. But on the off chance that the list is too long for you already, we can simplify it a bit by offering a simple dichotomy, a list with only two items. All decisions are either stochastic or deterministic (or a mixture; sorry, life is complicated).

Decision making can be equated to problem solving, and effective decisions come about because the problem is correctly understood. It is critically important to begin any decision process by first analyzing the situation into the two possible types: deterministic (linear, causal) or stochastic (dynamic, probabilistic).

is one in which the action and outcome certain inputs, certain outputs certainly ore, you will improve your cardiovascular health—no doubt. A stochastic process, on the other hand, is a process in which the outcomes are probabilistically rather than deterministically related to the actions taken. If you exercise more, you won't necessarily lose weight because you may eat more as a consequence. In stochastic situations the outcomes are uncertain, but they are available to analysis (often statistical analysis), and thus one can predict with varying degrees of probability what will happen, which, given a clear set of goals means one can deliberately select a course of action even though one can't be certain of the outcome, to say nothing of the consequences of that outcome.

Here's a simple contrastive example. Your bank account is deterministic; the national economy is stochastic. If you are like most people, from month to month you know how much is going in and how much is coming out of your personal bank account. The national economy, on the other hand, is dynamic in the sense that the factors that contribute to it contribute different amounts from month to month, which factors are relevant and how relevant they are is debatable. With so many dynamic factors contributing to the "bottom line," there really is no bottom line. It's more like there are bottom lines and various ways of interpreting each of them.

In both stochastic and deterministic decision situations, the less well you know the actual process involved (as compared to how you *think* the thing works) the less accurate your predictions will be. What looks to a novice like a stochastic situation might be a deterministic one to an expert. More often, however, the reverse is true. People who aren't familiar with something or have never done it may think it is simple because the people they have seen doing it make it look easy. Discerning subtle differences takes knowledge and experience, and absent that, we tend to vastly oversimplify and underestimate. In other words, ignorance and impatience tends to falsely convince us that the stochastic is deterministic.

While we may prefer deterministic processes because they offer a more vivid illusion of control, most significant decision situations are stochastic (dynamic and probabilistic). You can do considerable damage to yourself and others by reducing a stochastic decision to a deterministic one. Either/or thinking is one heuristic that people use to reduce a truly stochastic to an apparently deterministic situation. Narrow framing, or tunnel vision, is another. For more on how to avoid either/or deciding, see item 6 under the elaborated stochastic decision making process.

The worst mistakes are typically made when people predict with certainty an outcome that will in fact be influenced by random or unknown events. If you are certain Plan A will work, you are much less likely to have a Plan B, which means you're in much deeper trouble when Plan A fails. The only thing worse than being wrong is being blindsided.

Rule 15: Don't apply deterministic thinking to stochastic situations

Your Turn

1. Provide at least one example for each of the different kinds of decisions explained above. Save your examples of the deterministic and stochastic situations for the next two questions.

2. Make a list of deterministic decisions. How do you know that each action is causally linked to its outcome?

3. Make a list of stochastic decisions. What are the complexities in each case that make something other than a causal link between action and outcome inevitable?

4. Before we move on, see if you can add to my list of decision types.

5. If you are bored, look up the concept of "wicked problems."

Immediate, near-term, and far-term decisions

Whenever we make a decision it is because we want to solve a problem or obtain something we can't get directly. The object of our intention is called a "goal." A goal is a single answer to two linked questions: what and when. Goals are immediate, near term, or far term.

Immediate goals are like itches that need scratching or fires that need putting out: well-defined, unambiguous, discrete problems with obvious causes and predictably effective solutions. They are deterministic, in other words. You know what to do and how to do it. You also know when to do it because when is now. Action taken, problem solved. Complications arise when you mistake a complex decision situation for an itch that needs scratching. Taking immediate and focused action to solve a problem you don't fully understand creates new problems.

Unlike immediate goals, near-term goals, what you need to accomplish this semester or this financial quarter, can't be achieved with a single move and thus require sequencing your activities and prioritizing your resources (time, energy, money, etc.). To accomplish a near-term goal you need to set targets. A target is typically some kind of deliverable, a document, a skill set, a product, a number. Your targets should be concrete, specific, and stable. Moving targets are hard to hit. Conflicting targets, goals that are somehow in each other's way, seriously hamper success.

Because short-term goals can be achieved or abandoned quickly, temporarily shifting resources from longer-term projects and ignoring one or two of your immediate needs may provide enough resources to accomplish a short-term goal without harming your long-term plans or permanently changing your daily habits. If a short-term goal is proving illusive and therefore starting to siphon resources from longer-term goals or interfering significantly with immediate needs, then it's time to reassess the target or consider shifting the goal from short to longer term. If you respond to every instant message the moment it arrives, it will take you much longer to finish the spreadsheet you need to send out today by 2:00 pm.

Rule 16: You can't hit two targets with one arrow

Here is an example of a near-term goal decision-making process. Imagine you're just restarting an exercise regimen after years of inactivity. Putting "run a sub 8-min mile" on a calendar three months hence (just setting a goal) isn't helpful because you haven't decided how to get from today to three months hence. A more helpful approach is to work out a specific plan of exercise for each day between now and three months from now, increasing the intensity and duration a little bit each day. The first day's target is simply to park in the far lot and walk the extra distance. The next day's target is to take the elevator from the third floor after having walked in from the far lot. On day three, take the elevator from the fifth floor and walk a block after work. Day four, stairs plus walk 1.5 blocks and jog-walk the remaining half. Each time you hit a target you are that much closer to your goal.

Small wins are critical motivators, so set your first targets close by and then stretch them out a bit going forward.

Your Turn

1. One way to practice near-term decisions is to use a calendar. Pick a goal that might be accomplished in a month. Place that goal on day thirty-one of the month represented below. Then work back to day one, placing targets at regular intervals. Once you've got a plan, see if you can achieve it. Next month, try another one. Start small because easy victories are still victories and every win encourages further commitment. If you don't achieve your goal, pick something different or something similar but less ambitious and give it another shot. If a month seems daunting, pick a smaller goal and lay the targets down over a week. Conversely, pick a bigger goal and give yourself three months' worth of targets. Whether you chose a close by, near-term goal or a slightly further, near-term goal, what you are practicing is the disciplining of your experiencing self. Because the experiencing self has only immediate experience to go on, the planning self can trick it into following a longer path, one immediate sensation after another, until a target that was too far down range for immediate experience when the planning self set it comes immediately into view.

Sunday	Monday	Tuesday	Wednesday	Thursday	Friday	Saturday
			1	2	3	4
5	6	7	8	9	10	11
12	13	14	15	16	17	18
19	20	21	22	23	24	25
26	27	28	29	30	31	

Targets versus objectives

While it is possible to achieve near-term goals by setting targets, long-term goals typically require a less focused and more flexible decision-making process: a flashlight rather than laser beam. A lot will happen over the course of several months, to say nothing of years or decades. For one thing, over time you will be distracted by more immediate and therefore more apparently urgent needs. Additionally, short-term goals will come and go, constantly shifting your focus and temporarily altering your available resources. Crucially, over time you will change intellectually and socially and so the person who realizes a lifelong dream almost certainly will not be the same person who set that goal ten years earlier. This is why enjoying the process is so much more important than achieving specific goals in life and why some people prefer to make big decisions by intuitive thought processes rather than analytical ones. Obviously, if you don't know what you want you're unlikely to get it, but if you focus too closely, you are almost certainly going to miss the mark even as you hit your targets. Thus when setting long-term goals, it's often best to think in terms of a range of possible outcomes instead of focusing on a target or even a set of targets. Rather than deciding at fifteen, for example, that you want to be a doctor, it would be more prudent to develop a passion for science and biology and see where your passions take you.

Thus when it comes to long-term decision making, think objectives instead of targets. A target is concrete and static. An objective is abstract and dynamic. Targets are like individual stones on a specific path. Objectives are more like a bearing or heading. If having a million dollars when you retire is a target, minimizing expenses, maximizing savings, and consistently increasing investments are objectives. For most people, a million dollars is too far off to be realized without concerted and consistent repeated efforts along various lines, meaning that many apparently unrelated decisions will actually contribute to or conflict with your long-term goal. Your chances of scratching and winning a serious nest egg are vanishingly small. Because objectives are abstract, they can advise you how to respond effectively in any situation, even unforeseen situations. Objectives create values and preferences that eventually turn into habits of mind. Your habits of mind will always lead you to prefer what will contribute the most to your long-term goal or minimize the damage done to your progress when a setback is unavoidable. By setting objectives and letting them become cognitive habits, you turn a constantly deliberate decision situation into an unconscious decision situation.

If your goal is to make money, then any decision should be based on a highly positive return on investment (ROI) analysis. Your objective in such cases is always to look for and choose high ROI opportunities. If your primary objective is to enjoy your work, on the other hand, then a low ROI won't dissuade you. Indeed, if playing the piano or acting fascinates you, the really small ROI won't bother you at all—unless of course you want to get rich playing the piano, in which case your goal and your objectives are misaligned and the chance of disappointment enhanced.

Rule 17: For long-term goals, choose objectives over targets

If you are having trouble identifying your objectives, start with a compelling target, something you want, and then ask yourself what it is about that target that is consistent with your current values. If what you value doesn't align with the target, then either you don't want what you think you want or you need to reassess your values.

Your Turn

The essential take away from this section is that near-term and long-term goals typically require different decision processes. Targets need to be precise and truly relevant. Objectives need to be adaptive and dynamic value systems.

1.   Make a list of things you would like to accomplish, experience, or have (a set of goals).

2.   Now sort the list in terms of how long it will take you to achieve them, from shortest to longest.

3.   Which ones require targets?

4.   Which ones require objectives?

5.   Now see if you can turn the objectives into values.

When setting goals in general, at least beyond satisfying immediate needs and putting out spontaneous fires, beware the optimism bias. Caused largely by the experiencing self overestimating the planning self's capacity to get work done and avoid distractions and remain focused no matter what transitory needs come up, the optimism bias leads us to overestimate what we can accomplish while underestimating how long it will take and how much it will cost. Basically, add 20 percent to the cost and time required for personal projects and more to group projects. The greater the damage caused by failure, the greater the need to have sufficient slack built into the process to accommodate cost and time overruns. The optimism bias is helpful in that it will make you commit to projects that you might shy away from if you looked at them more ultimately worthwhile. Just as there's always a downside, there's always an upside. So plan boldly from the beginning. Just build contingencies into the process.

Summary

Each kind of decision calls for a different decision process. For example, using a fully deliberate process on a pseudo decision situation is a serious waste of time. Unless part of your deliberate process includes analyzing the situation to identify a significant difference among at first glance interchangeable options, there's no point in agonizing over which interchangeable option to choose. Similarly, if two things are completely different then comparing them as a way of preferring one to the other is pointless without a common denominator. If you want a piece of fruit, you can successfully compare an apple to an orange, but if the category of fruit isn't available for some reason or, more likely, it doesn't occur to you, then comparing apples to oranges is just dithering, a pointless form of pseudo deciding.

Just as you need to consider the decision type, the situation in which the decision is being made, the context, also needs consideration. Our decision styles have a tendency to change over time. Sometimes the time interval is moments or minutes. The instant someone cuts you off in traffic you feel like nothing matters so much as expressing wildly articulate one-fingered outrage. Three seconds later, if you are a fairly stable person, you will be singing along to the radio or tut-tutting over some news story, the insult long gone from consciousness. Most people can learn to count to ten, in other words, to know that a brief moment's reflection or even just waiting for a few seconds will change a decision situation and therefore afford a better or at least less impulsive decision. Thing is, often we don't even think to count to ten. We just decide and go when we might have been better off slowing down and thinking about what to do. What follows is the intellectual equivalent of a speed bump. (Don't give me the finger.)

How our brains work

So far we've been talking about decision making as though the organ we use to make decisions, our brain, is a necessary but invisible part of the process. We took the concepts of unconscious, semiconscious, and deliberate for granted. Just as it's possible to ride a bicycle blissfully unconscious of the physics involved, so it is possible to make sound decisions without taking psychology into account. Indeed, from the Enlightenment up until the relatively recent past (forty years or so), psychology has been ignored in the discussion of decision making on the grounds that our minds are like muscles that need merely to be disciplined in order to work correctly. Properly trained people make purely rational decisions, it was assumed. We don't tend to accept this assumption any more. Let me explain.

Many hundreds of years ago, the Greek philosopher Plato described humans as being like charioteers trying to control two horses, one less obedient, more impulsive, and stronger than the other (Plato 1995, 253c). Each of us is tasked with keeping our chariot on the road by disciplining our impulsive beast to follow the lead of our diligent horse. The metaphor of the two-horse chariot was a way of talking about reason and desire, impulse and deliberate action. The idea that we oscillate between these two poles has dominated discussions of thinking and living (decision making) ever since. For many years it was thought, as Plato thought, that the good life was possible only when the good horse dominated, when reason controlled passion. Rational actor theories of decision making, as they are sometimes called, assume that people will choose what is in their own best interests and that they know what their interests are. On this view of decision making, what everyone needs is accurate information, preferably in quantifiable form, and the willpower and intellectual discipline to think clearly and act rationally. Logic and computation can triumph over passion and only the weak or the simpleminded (and the young) fall victim to their passions. If you want to become a good decision maker, focus on the numbers, learn to quantify first and qualify later. Do the math. Find a way to quantify complexity so that it can be handled by logic and statistics.

Since the end of the Enlightenment blind faith in reason (a splendid oxymoron) has abated. Even the most traditional books about deciding have started to bracket their rational actor models of deliberative thinking with talk about psychology, cognitive biases in particular. Recent insights gained by neuroscience and psychology, to say nothing of the ubiquity of computer technology, have made the mind-as-computer metaphor more compelling than the psyche-as-charioteer metaphor. On this view, our minds operate on many different levels that don't directly communicate with each other. Think of it this way, computers have circuit boards with routines baked in that respond to streams of ones and zeros. These streams of ones and zeros are machine language. Above machine language you have an assembly language that acts as a go-between for the circuit boards and the rest of the hardware. Above that you have an operating system controlling memory allocation and coordinating the input and output devices. And above that you have the user interface, most typically these days a metaphorical desktop. Most computer users function almost exclusively on the desktop level, becoming aware of the operating system only when they misplace a file or when the operating system doesn't recognize a peripheral.

For intuitively inclined thinkers, the levels below the operating system are completely mysterious. Without them we can't do anything, but knowledge of them isn't relevant to our daily activities. For the more analytically inclined, knowledge of the systems below the operating system is thought to be important. It isn't necessarily true that the analytically minded truly understand what's happening below the desktop. Most analytical types have only a partial understanding and some will have a false understanding. Only the people who designed a given circuit board knows how it works all the way down. Our mind-as-computer metaphor hits a metaphysical vein right there, which you can ponder or ignore, as you like.

Whether we incline toward intuition or analysis, we all have routines running deep in our brains that keep our blood flowing and our lungs expanding and contracting and our hearts beating. These are autonomic reactions over which we have no conscious control. One level up from the direct experience of these sensations, we have interpretations of them. We call these interpretations feelings. While changes in our internal states give rise to sensations we are keenly aware of almost immediately, often we aren't quite sure how to interpret the sensations. We know we're feeling something but we aren't quite sure what because very similar sensations might be indicative of different states. "My heart is pounding. It that lust or exhilaration or exertion or panic or monosodium glutamate?" If you had some way to monitor your oxytocin and vasopressin and adrenalin (and MSG) levels, you might be able to clearly differentiate among similar arousal states. But of course we have no way to monitor our internal states at a chemical level. We just have the socially constructed analogues we call feelings. Finally, we have cognition, explanations based on the representations and models of reality that our minds produce. We don't directly interact with either our internal or the external world but rather with our models of them. These models are created by our brains but are outside our conscious awareness: as the desktop is to the circuit boards so the mind is to the brain, even for the analytical, hypercomputational types among us.

As a result, none of us fully understands what he or she is doing. Consciousness is largely a fictional construct, the byproduct of our minds doing what our minds do best, creating a coherent narrative out of a fractional subset of the available data.

David Eagleman puts the situation this way: "The conscious mind fabricates stories to explain the sometimes inexplicable dynamics of the subsystems inside the brain. It can be disquieting to consider the extent to which all of our actions are driven by hardwired systems, doing what they do best, while we overlay stories about our choices" (2011, 148). He goes on to assert with even greater emphasis that "our thoughts are generated by machinery to which we have no direct access" (193). And later he asserts that "much of who we are remains outside our opinion or choice" (199). That bears repeating: "Much of who we are remains outside our opinion or choice."

Timothy D. Wilson makes the mysterian claim a little less intensely: "Much of what we want to know about ourselves resides outside of conscious awareness" (2004, 3). Wilson believes that much of what we might call intuition, "judgments, feelings, motives" (8), happens outside of consciousness for the same reason an athlete who becomes aware of her body at the moment when she needs flawless execution will choke. To succeed on the field you have to get out of your mind, as the sports psychologists say. The more aware you are of some cognitive routines, the slower you will perform them and the greater the risk of failing to perform them at all. There is an important implication here, one you might want to reject but that you should nevertheless consider however briefly: if you don't have direct access to your judgments and feelings and motives, then trying to articulate them, to reflect on what's happening below consciousness, distorts or at least translates one form of cognition into another. What we feel and what we say we feel are not the same thing. More astonishingly, our motivations are not directly available to our minds either. We think we know why we are doing what we are doing, but really we don't.

The psychologist George Miller put it this way: "It is the result of thinking, not the process of thinking, that appears spontaneously in consciousness" (1962, 71).

If it is true that there are cognitive processes happening outside consciousness that nevertheless influence our decisions even though we don't know what they are doing, then we never make entirely deliberate decisions: we are not purely rational actors. At the very least, we don't understand our motivations or our actions as thoroughly as we might naively imagine we do. If this is even close to true, then rationalization and justification are much closer to deliberation than rational actor models mislead us into thinking.

While pondering the complexity and diversity of our mind/brain universe is a fascinating exercise, when it comes to decision making there's no immediate utility to the theorizing. If we have no access unaided by scientific inquiry into the workings of our mind/brain, what non-academic difference does it make what's going on in there?

Well, for one thing realizing how little we know about how we know helps restrain overconfidence, the single most common source of erroneous judgments. Moreover, we have quite a bit of evidence to support the idea that while the deeper regions may be beyond our consciousness we can nevertheless train our intuitions to respond accurately and unconsciously to specific situations, for example, when hitting a ball or playing a sonata or putting out a fire or differentiating attacking warplane blips on a radar screen from ground clutter and anomalies (Klein 1999). We can, in other words, develop expertise that enables us to offload some cognitive activity to the intuitive parts of our minds, thus freeing consciousness for the unique and the anomalous or even just the more pleasant. If you are a writer, for example, the more automatic your spelling, punctuation, grammar, and syntax, the more time you can spend on developing and organizing content. The same is true for arithmetic and all of the foundational intellectual practices. The less time you need to ponder the necessary, the more time you have to achieve the extraordinary.

Although pondering the problem of consciousness and the role that consciousness plays or fails to play in decision making doesn't help us make better decisions, it makes us more aware of how complex our thought processes are. Knowledge of this complexity makes us more reflective, which means that we have a powerful tool for shifting out of the autopilot of the experiencing self.

Here is another switch for your autopilot.

Behavioral economics, a branch of decision-making theo   ie famous by psychologists Amos Tversky and Daniel Kahnemar   es that we have essentially two systems of mind, sometimes c   l, for the sake of simplicity and to avoid semantic confusions caused by more common, baggage-carrying terms (reason, emotion), System 1 and System 2 (Kahneman 2013, 21). System 2 quantifies, calculates, and uses logic to draw valid inferences from available information. It uses working memory and concentration to question assumptions and verify apparent results. System 2 is capable of meta-cognition, thinking about its thinking practices, and it is therefore reflective and skeptical, which means it is also slow. In a nutshell, System 2 is slow but accurate and precise. It also takes a great deal of energy to operate and as a result we are often slow to invoke it, preferring the fast-thinking System 1 instead.

System 1 is associative, intuitive, and unconscious. It's the autonomic nervous system responding to internal and external stimuli, blood pressure, hormone secretion, and so on but also environmental data, the weather, light, movement on the periphery of vision, scents, and sounds, microfacial expressions, and such. System 1 also relies on patterns, cultural expectations, and habits of mind and cognitive heuristics to produce attitudes and orientations that indirectly and unconsciously help us make decisions. The two systems are unaware of each other. Indeed we only know of System 1 by way of observation from fMRI (functional magnetic resonance imaging) and inferences from controlled psychological experiments, which suggest, for example, that a split second before conscious thought kicks in, our minds have already inclined us in a specific direction. A common and powerful example is *priming*, in which putting a number or an idea in a person's head influences his next thought even though he is completely unaware of the influence and will in fact deny it if asked. Another common example is *the mere exposure effect*, in which a person's ideas are influenced to accept something simply because something different but similar has been a part of her unconscious mental landscape for a while without causing harm or suggesting the potential for harm and so has been accommodated into a general sense of well-being. While advertisers use both priming and the mere exposure effect to influence our decisions, by surreptitiously getting in our heads, as it were, they are not examples of the thoroughly debunked idea of subliminal advertising. They are simply exploiting our System 1's bias in favor of anything already present in our environments regardless of its actual value or any value our conscious efforts could attach to it. Our impulse toward disgust works similarly. The impulses of attraction and repulsion do not require training and indeed retraining them to accommodate different ideas is extremely taxing. If you don't believe me, and you were raised in the western hemisphere, try eating a durian fruit sometime. If you were raised in the eastern hemisphere, try eating a chocolate bar.

System 1 is fast but error prone because it is non-reflective and therefore overconfident. It also spontaneously creates coherence out of any data given, even observing patterns that don't exist (like faces on toast) and will if necessary manufacture data, using the memory or imagination to supply missing information or amalgamate contradictions. System 1 also disregards ambiguity. All of these traits make us feel smart and in control, which is why we are slow to invoke System 2. In fact there that happiness and feelings of contentm System 1 while System 2 is depressing (Kahneman, 114).

The errors to which System 1 are prone are known as cognitive biases, and the list of them is growing as research data accumulates (Kahneman, 20).[3] Some of these biases sound like logical fallacies. Social proof, for example, sounds a great deal like the bandwagon effect. Certainly their explanations are very similar. The difference between a logical fallacy and a cognitive bias is that while you can learn to avoid logical fallacies, you can't completely eliminate cognitive biases because they reside deep beneath consciousness and are not available to language; they are baked into the circuit boards of our brains. We can learn to recognize situations in which cognitive biases may be coming into play and so force ourselves to kick on System 2 as a way of double-checking the results offered by System 1, but that's the best we can do, and it will only be possible in situations where we have time and the inclination to think.

If you argue that something is true because everyone around you thinks it's true, then you are employing the logical fallacy of the bandwagon. On the other hand, deciding to go along with the crowd can sometimes make intuitive sense. If you are trying to find your way out of a stadium after a game, for example, follow the crowd. Similarly, if you are looking for a good restaurant, it would be reasonable to intuit from a long lineup outside the door that there's good food inside, while the place next door with just the one miserable looking person pushing food around on his plate maybe isn't such a good bet. In situations where the available evidence is sufficient for a conclusion, or time constraints eliminate the option of analysis, System 1 can generate plausible results quickly. So invoking System 2 in such settings would seem like overkill and indeed invoking it could generate

---

3. Kahneman points out that "System 1" and "System 2" are merely useful fictions, not accurate descriptions of how our brains work. They are a kind of shorthand that makes the argument he wants to make more readily intelligible (2013, 28).

nerdy distortions. Let's re-think our where to eat decision point using System 2 this time: "Both places provide food. Assuming the empty place isn't serving tainted food, maybe the service will be quick and the quiet space conducive to rumination. If the food tastes bad, I will eat less of it and fewer calories are better than too many for modern urban dwellers. Even if I get sick at least I'll be able to say I didn't jump on the bandwagon."

Rule 18: Don't accept System 1 solutions to System 2 problems

Knowing what the cognitive biases are and how they incline our decisions doesn't eliminate their power over our decisions. And that's a good thing, according to current thinking, because turning them off would make us so deliberate as to be incapable of making decisions at all. There is a fascinating cognitive test of what is called the somatic marker hypothesis (Brand et al. 2007) that seems to demonstrate a connection between emotion and judgment and thus decision making. If you're interested, have a look at "Emotion, Decision Making and the Orbitofrontal Cortex" (Bechara, Damasio, and Damasio 2000).

The most deliberate decisions are made by people who are fully aware (to the extent that's possible; Eagleman 2012; Wilson 2004) of when their cognitive biases may be leading them too quickly to a decision and capable of slowing down or even building into their practices the time and space for reflection that a System 2 answer requires (remember trigger decisions from the first section?). System 2 decision-making takes discipline and practice, an appreciation for numbers, an understanding of statistics (and common statistical errors), as well as a knowledge of human behavior that enables judgment based more on reasoned expectations and less on hope, prejudice, and default ideas about the world. System 2 can also require crafting an environment that can restrain System 1 from temptation. If you need to quit drinking alcohol, you need to stop going to bars and unfriend your drinking buddies. If you need to quit smoking, you need to find a less harmful cognitive break/reward mechanism (cookies are only a temporary alternative, sadly). Read Thaler and Sunstein's *Nudge* (2008) for a thorough explanation of how System 2 results can be coded into System 1 day-to-day living arrangements by means of what they provocatively call "libertarian paternalism." Let me give you a less vicious example. I was sitting at a red light the other day, a car in front of me and one behind me. There were no cars on the cross street. Suddenly, before the light turns green, the car in front takes off and runs the light. Eyebrows raised, I'm sitting there puzzling, when the car behind me pulls around me and runs the light. Now I'm thinking, foot hovering over the accelerator, "Maybe the light's broken; maybe something's coming up fast behind us; maybe, uh, maybe, I don't know." I'm searching for a rationalization to warrant my following them in breaking the simplest law we have. They did it. I want, I need, to do it too. But by then the light had turned green and I didn't have to jump on their bandwagon.

In that example, my System 2 kept my System 1 in check, at least for the three seconds it took for the light to turn green. I might not have lasted another two seconds. The two systems were working against each other. And this is often how people think about them, that System 2 is there to keep System 1 from having the third tequila shot and running off to Aruba with the bartender. But it may also be the case that System 1 can rightly but indirectly inform System 2. Here's a simplistic example.

Like a lot of people I have a dish by the door into which I throw my keys and whatever else I have in my pockets when I get home. A couple of months back I tossed a USB drive in the dish. Every day I grab my keys on the way out the door, and every day when I look in the dish of random stuff I focus instantly on the keys because that's my goal when I look in the dish and I ignore all the other stuff. Such is how our attention functions. It filters the intentionally irrelevant out of our perceptions. For the past few weeks, as I've been driving to work, I've been thinking it's time to update my playlist, which in my car is done by putting music on a USB drive and uploading it. As a contextual thinker, I forget about the playlist the minute I get out of the car. For the past few weeks as I've grabbed my keys out of the dish, I've found myself looking briefly and uncomprehendingly at the USB drive. I just see it every morning. No connection, just observation. And then yesterday as I'm thinking about associative thinking, it hits me, it's as if my unconscious mind is trying to reach my conscious mind by bringing the USB drive into the field of my vision. It wasn't until I made the connection that I remembered to take the drive with me and make a conscious note to self to copy some music to it.

Rule 19: Pay attention to what you aren't thinking

Because our System 1 processes are part of our limbic system, the oldest part of our brains in an evolutionary sense, and because System 1 is fast and often satisfying, there's likely some benefit in learning how to kick System 2 into gear. I'm not suggesting System 2 is in all cases preferable, nor am I suggesting that if the following puzzles don't puzzle you at all that you have superior decision-making skills. Both systems are equally important. It's just that most of us spend so much time exclusively in System 1 that we don't stop to think if the answers that seem to present themselves to us are really correct. As Kahneman takes pains to point out, the speed of System 1 will often lead to mistakes that System 2 will correct if only we will take the time to question our first impressions, our intuitions, and our prejudices.

Your Turn

Here are some puzzles to see if you can catch System 1 at work when it should be asleep.

1. If a ball and bat cost $1.10 together, and the bat is $1.00 more than the ball. How much does the ball cost? (See Kahneman 2013).

2. "People got sick. They ate spinach. Therefore, spinach made them sick." Logical or illogical? (See Fung 2010, 40).

3. If it is true that "almost all terrorists are Muslims," is it also true that "almost all Muslims are terrorists?" How about, are the expressions "no evidence of disease" and "evidence of no disease" equally valid? (For more on that particular error, see Taleb 2007).

4. You are walking down a dirt road searching for the village of Truth. You come to a fork in the road and realize that down one path is the village of Lies while down the other is the village of Truth, but you don't know which path leads where. A villager is standing at the fork in the road. You can ask him only one question. What question will set you on the path to Truth? (Adapted from Lieberman 2008, 27).

Summary

Essentially any answer that leaps quickly to mind may be a System 1 error, the result of a cognitive bias or the application of a deterministic way of thinking in a stochastic situation. This does not mean that all intuitive decisions are wrong, just that intuition and logic and math are not the same processes, not for most people at any rate. I know a number of people who think of themselves as System 2 default-type people, highly analytical and computational folks, who are also in fact highly competitive, even aggressive, and will push to win an argument thinking they are System 2 right to do so when they are also clearly being driven by System 1 impulses, the need to dominate. Thought processes can be simplified—and even, in some specific cases, optimized (in game theory, for example)—but that does not necessarily lead to *better* decisions. You have to know what *better* means, and of course it means different things in different settings and what is best now may be less so in the future. How many CDs do you have? Do you still have an iPod? What about a television?

There are a number of different expert opinions about the relationship between System 1 and System 2. Some people hold that System 1 needs to be restrained and that System 2 should rule. Others argue that System 1 is powerfully useful in critical situations. A third option is that System 1 can be trained to operate almost like System 2, offering speed and accuracy. A fourth option is that they are inseparable but operating at odds, sometimes one leading, sometimes the other. A more radical position, perhaps, is that System 2 produces merely fictional explanations for the unknowable decisions made by System 1. And finally, I suppose, one could argue that System 2 is largely useless, confined, as it is too small, purely formal problems that have little to do with life in "the real world."

Your Turn

1. Lay the preceding paragraph out on a continuum, all System 1 on the left and all System 2 on the right, with the various different mixtures in between. Add any that you can think of that I left out.

2. Where do you tend to fall on that continuum?

3. Explain the relationship between System 1 thinking and the experiential self we talked about in the introduction to this book?

4. Have you ever made a decision that surprised you, a kind of "Wow, I'm going to do this?" sort of decision? If so, can you surface the unconscious thought process that led to it? If you don't have the experience personally, can you find someone who has and listen to him or her surface that decision?

Evaluating decisions

So far we've been talking about how decisions are made (notice the passive voice?) and pondering the possibility that our decision processes are not always as rational as we might like to believe. We have noticed that intuitive processes are valuable in some settings (the intuitive is not irrational), and we have recognized that different decision situations are better suited to different decision processes. Thus we can conclude that we need multiple decision styles, some unconscious, some conscious, and some highly analytic and fully deliberate. We have also no⟍   ⟍textual and social factors influence how we make decisio⟍   ⟍/brain doesn't function in isolation.

Let's turn no⟍   ⟍ about how we evaluate decisions.

Pragmatism is the idea that we can evaluate a decision based on the value of its outcome. If we did X and we got Y and we wanted Y or we like the consequences of Y, then X was a good decision. This thought process assumes that X caused Y. Assuming a causal link where there isn't one is a common logical error. If we wore a ring when we won the game, then wearing "the lucky ring" means winning the game. Superstition is a weak deliberative process. If X doesn't cause Y, then associating X and Y positively or negatively is a flawed System 1 kind of error.

In deterministic decision-making settings, pragmatism works because the outcome can be clearly linked to the actions that led to it; thus a bad outcome means a flawed process and a good outcome means a correct process. If there are stones in the clay, then the urn will crack when fired. If you drink seawater, you will get sick. But in stochastic situations, the outcome is complexly related to the process. Thus the outcome is an unreliable indicator of how well the process works. In such cases, even a series of successful outcomes may be misleading. Three homeruns in your first professional at bat does not a homerun record-breaking career predict.

Once we start to question the value of an outcome, or the consequences of it, or whether or not we should have wanted it in the first place, life gets too complicated for a deterministic decision-making process. Add to that set of complications the additional quandary of how one decision may lead to a place from which some options became possible and others cease to exist (a linked decision), and you get the kind of truly profound complexity that is real life.

One solution to the pragmatist's problem is offered by the parable of the Taoist farmer. A farmer's only son is playing in the field when he steps in a hole, twists his ankle, and breaks his leg. The other villagers run over to commiserate with the farmer. "Your only son!" they wail. "Horrible! You must be devastated." The farmer just nods and says, "It's too soon to tell." The villagers depart, some admiring his stoicism, others puzzled by his apparent lack of concern. A month later the boy is still on crutches when the local authority decides to conscript all able-bodied young men. "How lucky you are," say the villagers, "that your son will be spared." The famer just shrugs, "It's too soon to tell." The battle comes to the village and while everyone else is packing their belonging and running for cover, the old farmer has to help his son to safety, leaving everything else to plunder and ruin. The villagers commiserate, "Catastrophic! You've lost everything. How terrible." The farmer nods sagely and says, "You can carry this narrative on to my grave but even there you will have to admit that it's too soon to tell."

If you wait to see what happens next as a way of evaluating an event, you will need to suspend judgment indefinitely. It will always be too soon to tell until it's too late to tell anyone else. If we never know with certainty if an event will have good or bad consequences because all consequences have their own consequences from here to the grave, then pragmatism is impossible and the old farmer's quiet endurance (and perhaps beyond), born of permanently suspended judgment, is the only truly intelligent way to live.

Given that the outcome of a decision is rarely a discrete event but rather an event that leads to other events that may or may not be intended, given, in other words, that nearly all decisions are linked decisions, evaluating a decision based on the outcome is problematic. It is quite possible, for example, for a lifesaving operation to go exactly as planned and for the patient to die anyway.

An alternative to pragmatism is formalism, in which one evaluates a decision based on how well the decider made use of the information and resources available at the decisive moment, in pursuit of a specific goal, without concern for the value of the goal, the ramifications of the goal, or even for whether or not the goal was achieved. It's this formalist perspective that renders sensible the paradox of the successful operation that precedes (notice I didn't say *leads to* and thus imply causation) the patient's death.

If you take a formalist approach to decision making, then your focus is on taking the right steps irrespective of the outcome or its consequences. "I want E. I can get A, and A will necessarily lead to either B or C. From B I have a 60 percent chance of D and from C, an 80 percent chance. Therefore, I choose C because it gives me the best chance of getting D and from D, E will be within reach." Once the process is complete, you can test each link in the chain, but unless you are dealing with a purely causal decision situation, like dominoes falling, then the process, no matter how flawless, doesn't guarantee what happens in the end. The correct process correctly performed gives you the best chance of reaching your goal, but that's the best you can do, in stochastic situations at least. In the end, luck, random events, and unforeseen variables may influence the outcome, to say nothing of what happens next or how you feel about it. The process is what matters because the process can be controlled. The outcome doesn't matter because that can't be controlled. You pay your money, and you take your chances. Such is the formalist's perspective on evaluating decisions.

There's a fairly profound disagreement between those who champion the value of the bottom line (pragmatists) and those who focus exclusively on the means to a probabilistic outcome (formalists). We might call this the product versus process disagreement (or the lab coat vs. the white shirt and necktie struggle). Those who prefer to focus on processes argue that chance plays too large a part in the ultimate outcome for the value of a decision to be established only by whether or not the outcome was achieved. As the famous early statistician Jakob Bernoulli put it, "One should not appraise human action on the basis of its results" as quoted in Mlodinow, 19. Such an assertion will astonish the goal oriented among us, anyone for whom the phrase "proven track record" produces a nod of approval rather than a roll of the eyes.

If you are currently in the borderland between the pragmatists' and the formalists' camp, it's important to remember the distinction between stochastic and deterministic situations here, to appreciate the fact that some situations allow for processes that provide truly predictable outcomes while other situations are available to processes that have only probabilistic outcomes. We should also point out that while statisticians are steeped in probabilities and fascinated by uncertainty, their thinking is ultimately focused on getting the best possible view of the probabilities just before the dice land and the possible outcomes become a single result. Probabilistic thinkers aren't entirely indifferent to results, just less inclined to accept a deterministic view of the relationship between process and outcome.

Mlodinow articulates the process position very clearly when he asserts, "Although statistical regularities can be found in social data, the future of particular individuals is impossible to predict, and for our particular achievements, our jobs, our friends, our finances, we all owe more to chance than many people realize" (2008, 195). The process position appeals not only to the statistically minded among us but also, paradoxically, to those of us who don't like to think of ourselves as "mere statistics," those of us, in other words, who like to foreground subjective experience and background abstract ideas when trying to decide. There's a famous story about how President Harry Truman once demanded off microphone, "Someone find me a one-armed economist." Truman was tired of his advisors saying, on the one hand, this, but on the other, that. Process-oriented thinkers are keenly aware of nuances and uncertainties; they are probabilistic rather than deterministic thinkers. The pragmatic, product oriented among us are more inclined to double down and hope for the best, prepared to rationalize the positive outcomes as foreseen and justify the negative outcomes as unforeseeable or, better yet, to find some way to spin either to advantage.

While pragmatists accept that the efficacy of an outcome will validate the process that led to it, regardless of the process itself, formalists tend to evaluate the process on factors intrinsic to it regardless of the outcome. Formalists appreciate the elegance of a solution, parsimony being a chief value—the least number of steps required to accomplish a task. To a formalist, pragmatists look brutal.[4] Their goal is to solve the problem and once they have a workable solution, they move on. Often the preference for a formalist or a pragmatic approach should be dictated by the nature of the decision and the situation in which the decision has to be made. High-pressure, low-time, naturalistic situations require a pragmatic (and intuitive) approach. Well-formed, deterministic problems with clearly defined goals can be solved with formalistic approaches. Stochastic problems that can be determined, like those studied in game theory, can also be available to formalistic decision practices.

In the end, whether you are a process- or a product-oriented decision maker has a lot to do with your tolerance for uncertainty. If you find uncertainty distressing you may be inclined to oversimplify all

---

4. I once met a guy who sailed his forty-foot sloop from Liverpool to the Panama Canal, and when I expressed my admiration he said, "Not hard, really; you just sail south till the butter melts and then you turn right." That's pragmatism.

decision settings by thinking in black-and-white (either/or) terms and making habitual or conventional decisions—a bird in the hand is worth two in the bush. If, on the other hand, you enjoy uncertainty, you may prefer to take a wider view of your options and a more complex approach to evaluating them. By learning something of probability you may develop a taste for uncertainty or at least a greater tolerance for uncertain outcomes. For most people, there are some uncertainties we can live with and others we will seek to minimize. You need to figure out for yourself what your tolerance for uncertainty is and how it influences how you think in different situations. You may find that you need to increase your tolerance for uncertainty in order to improve your decision-making practices. If you can't increase your tolerance for uncertainty, then you might prefer to live in a world with fewer stochastic decision moments.

Rule 20: Don't think pragmatically about process-oriented decisions and vice versa

Your Turn

1. Are you typically a result- or a process-oriented decider?

2. If you consider yourself sometimes pragmatic and sometimes formalistic, can you identify the situations that lead you to prefer one method of assessment to the other?

3. Can you think of a decision during which you shifted from process to outcome or vice versa? What prompted that shift?

Summary for chapter 1

We've been through a lot by now so let's recap before we move on. We've noticed that each of us is composed of different selves, each with its own kind of decision-making process. Sometimes we think quickly and sometimes we think slowly, and sometimes the style and the decision match and sometimes they don't. While we are inclined to think that irrevocable decisions require ponderous processes, carefully worked out plans, we realize that life has a way of intervening over time and so we need to make our long-term plans in the most flexible ways possible, which means that intuition may play a part even in long-term decision situations. We've also noticed that there are different types of decisions and that each has to be thought about in slightly different ways, that logistical decisions are about how rather than why, for example, and that some decisions have consequences far outside the scope of the original decision, like when we get in the habit of drinking a 2,000-calorie mocha latte on a daily basis. We've also come to realize that some decisions are simple cause to effect situations and so can be dealt with in deterministic ways while others are complex and dynamic and so require predictive and probabilistic thinking. We've also observed that while targets are the best way to achieve near-term goals, objectives based on values are more likely to achieve longer-term goals.

The next chapter focuses on predictive and probabilistic thinking.

CHAPTER 2
Thinking Ahead

Foresight

Unconscious decisions are made in the present with the goal of satisfying immediate needs and as such they are the purview of the experiential self. The reflective self tends to step up when a decision seems to have gone wrong, either because it led to the wrong outcome or because the intended outcome was achieved but the consequences were problematic. The deliberate self, focused as it is on the future, needs ways to predict what will happen next.

Whenever we face a deterministic situation, looking ahead is relatively straightforward. "If I flip this light switch, I will wake the kids." "If I don't replace this five-year-old car battery soon, I will be stranded in the near future." "If I don't get a grip on my credit card spending, I'm going to have a financial problem two years from now, unless I win the lottery or inherit some money or daydream, daydream, daydream," as the experiential self-kicks the deliberate self offline.

Stochastic situations require a form of thinking that is more complex than mere cause to effect. Whenever other people are directly or indirectly involved in a decision, for example, you have to take what they will do into account. See the section on game theory for more about how others may affect decisions. While people are by no means cause to effect automatons, we are nevertheless predictable to the extent that we have observable habits and conventional ways of being.

Because most people spend as much time as they can on cruise control, they don't often deviate from their habits and inclinations, and thus if you are familiar with someone, you can anticipate her actions and even her feelings. If you know someone really well, you can interpret what he or she is thinking from just a few words or half phrases. People who have spent many hundreds of hours in each other's company know what the other is thinking without either saying anything. That's not clairvoyance; it's just shared context and familiarity.

You can even predict the behavior of people you don't know well because cultural norms and standard scripts dictate how we behave in specific situations. If you are on a multi-lane highway and a sports car races by you on the right, you don't need it to signal left for you to anticipate its diving in front of you on its way to the even faster lane. That's what sports car drivers do.

Researchers have found, to take a slightly less mundane example, that if you follow a request with a reason for making it, no matter how lame the reason is, you will more often get compliance than not. People similarly tend to respond to signs of authority by complying, signs of ambivalence by doubting and questioning, and signs of prestige by envy or admiration. Interpretive practices are predictable in this way and so can be used both to get people to make decisions go your way and to anticipate their next move, in the short term at least. Foresight is really just anticipating what will happen next, and it's only possible to the extent that norms, patterns, habits, and practices are regularly exhibited. Familiarity with people and situations and cultural norms leads to a clearer understanding of what's coming next.

The ability to infer from the context and a person's actions what another person is thinking is called "theory of mind." Some people seem to be better at this than others. Inferring another's mental state is not just about sympathy or empathy because it's possible to accurately infer what someone else is thinking without caring. Sociopaths, apparently, are especially good at this creepy sort of psychological calculus. (See Stout and Frasier 2005 and Dutton 2012 if you are interested in this sort of thing.) Some people are terrible at theory of mind. We use the term "autistic" very loosely to label people who seem completely stuck in their own heads, basically oblivious to others, or freaked out by them when they try to reach in. Normal, non-game-theoretic decisions that directly or indirectly involve other people will require some theory of mind.

Event horizons

When you need to decide in a situation in which other people's actions aren't directly related, you can still use patterns to anticipate the future and thus make informed decisions. In the simplest possible sense, you can see Christmas coming so you can readily decide to save some money for presents and feasts. You also know to buy next year's wrapping paper and plastic wreath the day after this year's Christmas. At New Year you will see endless top ten lists and ads for exercise equipment and diet guides as the remorse associated with over indulgence leads to New Year's resolutions and more of the same at the same time next year. So if you need to sell that StairMaster you hang clothes on, put it on craigslist January 2. The next generation of your favorite electronic device is only a product cycle away, a seemingly ever-shrinking span of time. Do you buy this one or wait for the next one? You can foresee your car depreciating before it starts disintegrating and so you can predict you will need the car payment money for repairs after the car note is paid off. If you buy a house that's fifteen years old, be prepared to replace the major systems and quite likely the roof in the next five years. The cost of an item includes not only the sale price but also the cost of ownership.

When a person relocates, which can be easily operationalized as "buys a house," it's fairly predictable that he will need to establish new relationships and discover new businesses, lawyers, doctors, restaurants, and so on. Realtors can easily predict this need and so they sell the address information of recent sales to local businesses, who in turn market their services to the new arrivals. When a person graduates from college, it's similarly possible to predict certain things about her. A move is likely, as are larger purchasing power, a new wardrobe, new friends, and so forth. The birth of a child, similarly, presents new experiences and needs as well as new fears and opportunities. This is of course why all the new parents in a neighborhood seek each other out and become a cohort through the school years, though of course some will move. There will be divorces and financial crises and big promotions that move some people out of the neighborhood even as others move in.

Our challenges and opportunities in our twenties are different from our challenges and opportunities in our fifties. While each of us has a unique perspective, the vast majority of us will go through the same events on more or less the same schedule, births, coming of age ceremonies, marriages, children, divorces, graduations, career advances and setbacks, decline, illness, and death. Some of us will arrive early for some events and others late and some will skip some standard destinations and others will deviate entirely from the norm, but for the most part every one of a class and time and country will have remarkably similar experiences. The regularity of event horizons means you can anticipate and prepare for possible futures even though you don't know for certain what your future holds. Such a sense of recurrence is difficult to embrace personally because we experience the world subjectively and this leads us to think we are different from everyone else. We are not that different. We are not above average. We are not exempt from statistical analysis. Thus identifying and acknowledging patterns is a critical part of decision making. While real patterns are helpful, however, apparent patterns are problematic.

The identification of patterns is thought to have been so important for human survival over the millennia that our brains have become focused on finding them, so much so in fact that we are capable of seeing them even where they don't exist, just as we see faces whenever we are presented with three dots on an ambiguous background. There's even a word for this phenomenon, *paternicity* (Shermer 2011). Actually, seeing patterns in random data is so common there are two words for it. *Apophenia* is the other. Take your pick.

One of the most common sources of erroneous patterns is a large data set and a pressing need to make sense of it. If you were to look at epidemiological data about the incidence of cancers around the United States, you would inevitably find a few small population centers with a high incidence of cancer and you might conclude there must be some carcinogen at work there. You might be right, but you very well might be wrong. Statistical variation alone could account for the difference. This effect is sometimes called the "sharpshooter effect." Fire a shotgun against a barn a few times and then draw a bull's-eye around the densest cluster of holes, and ta-da!, you're a sharpshooter. (For more, see *The Drunkard's Walk*.)

Just because something just got better or worse doesn't mean it will continue in that direction. The only way you can be certain you've identified a trend is if you can prove a causal link or a deeply engrained social convention. If you can find a covariance, one changes and so does the other, that too might be worth betting on. But random runs and false positives happen all the time. The world is more stochastic than our System 1 impulses want our current self to believe.

Rule 21: Decide what to do now based on an informed opinion about what's most likely to be coming next

Your Turn

1.   How far into the future can you see? What will you be doing next week, next month, next year? Where do you want to be

five years from now? What about ten? Try to be as specific as possible as you answer these questions. You might even use a template composed of specific areas of focus such as education, relationships, finances, location, occupation and skills, activities, hobbies, places you've visited, and maybe people you want to meet. Write each heading on a Post-it note and then place bullets under each heading. Focus on specific details.

Predictive analytics

Ubiquitous computing has provided a galaxy of data from which we are starting to glean patterns that seem to offer glimpses of specific futures. While it's still true that the world is more stochastic than deterministic, it seems that perhaps it is now possible to predict, not with certainty but with enough likelihood to make betting on the outcome possible, what a specific person might, say, purchase in the near future or whether he will default on a loan or fail to pay a credit card installment, whether she will cheat on her taxes and even if she is about to become or just recently became pregnant. If that last example creeps you out, you are not alone.

There's an infamous example of what the industry calls "predictive analytics," recounted by one of its luminaries, Eric Siegel (2013), and presented to the world for the first time by *New York Times* journalist and author Charles Duhigg. The man at the center of the media blizzard was Andrew Pole, a quant (data analyst) who was working at the time for Target. Pole designed an algorithm for predicting future purchases based on tracing past buying activities forward to the present. To test whether the tool could indeed predict a purchase, Pole told it to take a point-of-sale moment in the past for a customer and then, using purchases that preceded that date in the past, see if it could predict that specific past purchase. The testing suggested the predictive model worked reasonably well. Siegel asserts that the model "identified 30 percent more customers for Target" (2013, Kindle Locations 1322–1323). As Siegel explains, "Target pulled together training data by merging the baby registry data with other retail customer data, and generated a 'fairly accurate' predictive model. The store can now apply the model to customers who have not registered as pregnant" (Kindle Locations 1315–1317).

An outraged father whose teenage daughter, still living at home, received coupons for her then unborn baby started the snowstorm of criticism. Bad enough the father didn't know his daughter was pregnant. Neither did she, apparently, though in fact as it turned out she was. The father wrote a scathing letter to Target and word got out.[5] Target hadn't done anything wrong, but it had done something very spooky. It seemed to have predicted the future.

"Seemed" is the critical term here. Tarot card readers and psychics "seem" to predict the future by speaking in vague generalities chosen based on the appearance, age, dress, accessories, and demeanor of a client, refined slightly by the client's responses and modeled after common human experiences. The "prediction" is an illusion created by the client reading meaning into the vague words of the "psychic."

This is not what Target was doing, but its prediction was still in a sense an illusion that just happened to hit a bull's-eye that made the target explode, as it were. The trend spotted in the data suggested that a female customer who had bought the items the young woman in question bought would shortly join the baby registry, and so it assumed that a specific set of ads would likely pay off if she received them. Target hadn't predicted her pregnancy. They had predicted that a previously seen buying pattern might apply to a specific individual and so offered ads to her to nudge her next purchases. It is quite possible that the same set of ads landed in the inbox of many other women, some of whom were charmed by the serendipity and others who tossed them with a resounding *ppffft*. What Predictive Analysis enables is a far more sophisticated variation of the psychic's trick, using commonly applicable data to make plausible inferences. Companies with billions of sales transactions simply have far better data to work with than the average individual has.

And, and this is more important, most people live lives that are quite consistent with the lives of those in their generation, tax bracket, upbringing, religious affiliation, income, and so on. No one is so unique as our vivid subjectivity misleads us to imagine. We all live engrossed by our subjective impressions, but take a step back and clearly discernible patterns appear, patterns that enable statistically valid inferences of what's next for each of us. Think about it this way, even though it's absolutely true that your death isn't foretold, given enough information about your family history, your genetic

---

5. Siegel (2013) casts doubt on the veracity of the father-daughter story. The article in question was in the February 2012 *New York Times Magazine*. Whether the story is true or not, the fact is predictive analysis clearly has the capacity to identify specific individuals as more probably ready than not for a specific sales pitch, and on those occasions when the pitch lands squarely, there will be startled looks and even gasps if the audience isn't aware of the possibilities.

makeup, and your lifestyle, any life insurance company good enough to remain in business has your date down to within a year or two. The older you get, the closer its approximations get. Of course they don't literally have your personal date down. What they know is merely a statistical reality. Your date may be sooner or later. Their prediction isn't personal.

Another way to think ahead is to consider the implications of a rule, to see the logic of a situation. When you have a decision to make in a deterministic or basically deterministic setting—that is, when there are rules or tightly maintained conventions or when there's a logic in the sense that given some things, others almost always follow—you need to think through the implications of the rules. There's a famous puzzle called the Wason test. You are shown four cards like so.

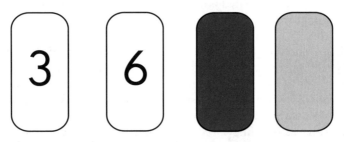

You are told that each card has a number on one side and a color on the other. What is the least number of cards you would need to turn over in order to test the asserted "rule" that if a card is grey on one side it has an even number on the other? The answer is two cards, the grey and the card with the number 6 on it. The blue card and the card with three don't fit the rule. If you struggled with that question, you are in good company. Roughly 75 percent of people fail this logic test. Now consider this example. Each of the four cards below represents a patron in a bar. On one side of each card is the patron's age and on the other what they are drinking. How many cards do you need to turn over to know if the drinking age has been violated?

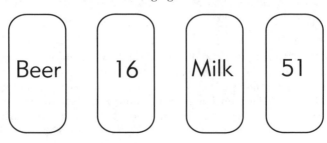

If you decided the answer is two cards, you are again in good company because most people get this test right. Curiously, both tests are logically identical but the second is much more often answered correctly because the implications of the rule are embedded in cultures in which alcohol is a popular controlled substance. Most of us are good at identifying cheaters; many of us are not so good at understanding the implications of rules in conditional logic puzzles. If you can represent a logical problem as a social one and the analogue is sound, then you may be able to discover that what you thought was stochastic is in fact deterministic, but you have to be careful you've really got an analogue and not just a tempting but erroneous substitution. For more along these same lines, you might want to read Gigerenzer (2013).

Regardless, don't just memorize the rules. Contemplate their implications. I have a parking permit that says, "The use of this permit by anyone other than the registered permit holder is prohibited." Obviously that rule means you aren't supposed to lend the permit to another driver. But what's the implication (the consequence) of the rule? At the bottom of the card the parking authority thoughtfully spells it out: "Registered permit holder is responsible for any citations issued to this permit." Rarely are the implications of a rule spelled out, and fortunes are to be had by people who discover unnoticed implications.

Rule 22: Don't just memorize the rules; ponder their implications

Your Turn

1. The entrance to a park near my house has a sign providing the rules and regulations of the park. Item three is "The park is open from sunup until sundown, every day." What is the implication of that rule? Over the course of the next day, pay attention to the rules and regulations signs you pass, next to the pool, for example, or at the parking garage, or at the park. And see if you can express the implication of each rule.

2.   Pick a simple game. List the rules. See if you can identify the implication of each rule as it gets played out in the playing of the game.

When you think ahead, anticipate what someone will do or what might happen next; you will likely think in terms of probabilities. "What are the chances that X will happen?" There are rules for that.

Probability

When it comes to thinking ahead, the most common practice is probability analysis. *Probability* has two meanings: what people expect will happen given a set of sometimes unwarranted assumptions (cultural norms, stereotypes, untutored intuitions) and the statistical likelihood of an event occurring. Our expectations are often unfounded and we all have cognitive tricks up our sleeves for dealing with unexpected outcomes, all of which make the first form of probability problematic. The second, numeric, form is a much more analytical way of determining what level of certainty we ought to have about a possible outcome. However, numeric probability requires quantification and we aren't always good at quantifying beliefs and values and desires, all of which contribute to how we think about what to do next.

While there isn't room in this short book to do justice to the topic (start by reading H. W. Lewis, *Why Flip a Coin?* (1997), the basic arithmetic in the basic examples of probability isn't all that difficult, just fractions, addition, and multiplication. There's no reason to shy away from probability. Indeed, as both Lewis (1997) and John Allen Paulos, author of *Innumeracy* (1988) assert, our culture's fear and loathing of basic probabilities and statistics is a source of disastrous social and economic problems, not to mention pseudo-science and investment swindles.

Let's look at a couple of lightweight examples to ease your mind if you find numeric probability daunting.

The basic rule is this:

The probability of an event is calculated by dividing each outcome by the total number of possible outcomes (aka, the "sample space")

If there are two possible outcomes, and nothing biasing the result, as is the case when you flip a standard coin, then the probability of the coin landing heads up (desired outcome) is .5, and therefore tails up (undesired outcome) is also .5. Flip an unbiased coin enough and you will see that on average you get an even split. You may see a run of heads or a run of tails, but that's just the nature of chance. Each individual flip of an unbiased coin offers a 50/50 chance of heads or tails. If you just flipped heads for the fifth time in a row, what are the odds of heads on the next toss? Still 50/50. Thinking that the probability must be less or more because of what has just happened is known as the gambler's fallacy. No toss influences another toss when it comes to unbiased coins. Discrete events have discrete probabilities. There are no linked decisions when it comes to tossing coins or throwing dice.

So one of the questions you have to ask yourself when considering the probability of an outcome is "Is this a coin toss or not; does the past influence the present probability in any significant way?" In games in which the circumstances change over time, like five-card poker, the immediate past does matter. If you have a 4/52 (one in thirteen) chance of drawing an ace the first time around, the chances of drawing a second ace on the very next draw is $4/52 \times 3/51$ because there's one fewer ace in the deck from which your next card is being drawn. If you do the math, you can see that your chances of drawing a natural four of a kind are 1/221 or roughly 0.0045 percent.

In games, for which the rules and situations are clearly defined and the available resources ultimately knowable, it's possible to calculate the odds with precision, which isn't the same thing as predicting the future by any means, but it gives you a numerical basis upon which to build analytical comparisons. Your chances of a straight (.382 percent) can be clearly compared to your chances of a flush (.197 percent).

In decision situations in which two events are mutually exclusive—that is, an either/or situation, or, when having one means not having the other—the probability of either happening is determined by adding the probability of each together. This is typically written as

$$P(A \text{ or } B) = P(A) + P(B)$$

Let's take another example from cards. You are about to turn over the first card from the top of a fresh deck. What are the chances it's either an ace OR a king? Well, the chances of an ace are 1 in 13. And the chances of a king are also 1 in 13. So the chances of the first card off the top of a fresh deck being EITHER an ace OR a king (no one card can be both) are 2/13.

In decision situations in which two events are nonexclusive—that is, an and/or situation—the probability is determined by adding the two individual probabilities that give you the OR and then determining the probability of an event that combines the two possibilities by subtracting that probability from the product. This is typically written as

$$P(A \text{ and or } B) = P(A) + P(B) - P(A \text{ and } B)$$

What are the chances of an ace OR a spade coming up off the top of a regular deck of cards? Keep in mind that among the aces there's the ace of spades, and among the spades, there's also the ace of spades.

$$P(A \text{ and or } B) = P(A) + P(B) - P(A \text{ and } B)$$

$$\text{Ace}(1/13) + \text{Spade}(13/52) - \text{Ace of Spades}(1/52) = \text{Ace or Spade}(4/13)$$

We have to subtract the ace of spades because we included it twice in the first calculations, once as the chances of an ace and once as the chances of a spade.

If flipping a coin once gives you a 50/50 chance of heads, what are the chances of five heads in a row? Resist the urge to jump to a conclusion: stand down, System 1. I'm not asking about the independent event of a single coin toss but a series of independent events falling in a specific pattern. The arithmetic here is P^N, the probability of each discrete event times the number of times you might see it turn out in a specific way. In this case, 2^5 or $2 \times 2 \times 2 \times 2 \times 2 = 32$. Therefore, the probability of five heads in a row is 1 in 32. (Toss a coin five times, 32 times in a row, and you will likely see it come up heads five times in a row just once.)

So if someone says, I'll give you 5 dollars if you can throw heads five times in a row, take the bet because you've got nothing to lose; just don't expect to win. If they wager you, the odds you want are 31 to 1. In that case the question you want to ask yourself is "How much do I want to pay for this bit of fun?"

As we've noticed, with games, carefully defined and resource- and variable-finite situations, it's possible to put a number on the chances of an outcome, but what about with decisions involving innumerable resources and variables? What are the chances that the next album by Lorde (or any recent hit maker you can think of) will also be a hit? Clearly, this question is complex and if you were in the position of deciding whether to back the next production or not, you'd have some complicated thinking ahead of you. Or you could deny the existence of complexity, insist that this is a causal rather than a probable situation, and go with the "proven track record" theory.

Let's decide not to oversimplify. We know from the gambler's fallacy that just because the last one was a hit (or a bomb) doesn't mean the next one will be. They are separate events. On the other hand, the talent and presence of the performer will likely remain the same between now and the next production. Lorde won't change. So the questions have to be about whether the next production has hooks that work as well as the last hooks worked and themes (and beats and chords) that speak so directly to the culture, whether the culture's interests remain the same or both change in the same way, and whether no one more compelling comes along. Wow. Not simple. How many times does a person have to win to be considered a winner? How many hits does a hit maker make? Does the fact that someone scored a hit the last time out increase, decrease, or leave unchanged the probability of the next shot hitting the mark? Were Lorde tossing coins, we could figure the chances precisely, P^N, but she isn't tossing coins; she's dropping tracks. If we were talking about someone with many years in the industry or even a few, then we might think that momentum will carry the day. Or that brand loyalty, a huge resource of die-hard fans, would ensure a hit regardless of the quality of the latest production. But there's only one effort out so far (as of this writing). And then there's the idea of the "sophomore slump," the tendency, imaginary or real I don't know (although that fact is knowable), for the second effort to flop. And then, we are assuming that quality of production directly affects sales, and that too is debatable. How many "hits" do you have in your collection from years past that when they come up now in your random rotation you shake your head and wonder, "Why did I buy that?"

When it comes to decisions for which ___ mathematically knowable, you would be f___ Lewis says, "You'll win more often than ___ with intelligence" (1997, 196). And in such cases, the math is pretty straightforward if you know the sample space because if you do, then the odds of an event happening are 1 divided by the sample space. In cases for which the number of variables affecting the outcome are too numerous or dynamic to be properly quantified, however, you have to consider whatever numbers you can come up with as contributing information rather than as deciding factors.

The more ways something can happen, the more likely it is to happen. This is why seven is a better bet than four when dice are involved (six ways to roll seven with a pair of dice compared with three ways to roll a four). But the more independent factors there are contributing to something happening or not, the harder it is to predict the outcome.

Rule 23: Don't confuse your expectations or your wishes with the actual probability of an outcome

Your Turn

1.   If there is a 10 percent chance of rain, will you cancel the picnic? What about a 30 percent chance? What happens to your thinking if instead of a 30 percent chance of rain you think there is a 70 percent chance of no rain?

2.   How many people would you need to gather to find one who has the same birthday as you? (If you want to look this up, it's commonly known as the "birthday problem." Turns out, by the way, that you get a 99.9 percent chance with just seventy people, but I asked you to find 1, i.e., to be certain.)

Conditional probabilities

Outside of games, in which the rules and variables regulate the outcomes, decisions get more complicated and the math thus becomes more complicated. In life most of the probabilities we encounter are conditional, meaning that our confidence in the probability of an outcome is influenced by other events or conditions either happening or not happening. The current thinking about how to deal with conditional probabilities descends from a man named Thomas Bayes (b. 1701, d. 1761), an English minister and mathematician.

Bayes was interested in how the occurrence of one event can shift your confidence (or degree-of-belief) in the occurrence of another indirectly related event. The basic thought pattern here is something like this: prior to anything else happening, how confident are you that B will happen? This is known as a "prior probability." Note that at issue is your *confidence* in the probability of an event happening, not the probability itself. The second element in this thought pattern is either the happening of a second event or the arrival of new information. Given that event A has just happened (or condition A has become known), now how confidently do you predict B? This second condition is known as a "posterior probability."

Let's be a bit more concrete. What are the chances of American driver A getting in a car wreck? Well, given just that little information, we would say the odds are roughly 1/40 million.

If there are 200 million licensed drivers in America and 5 million accidents in a given year, then the odds of a licensed driver getting in an accident in that given year are 1/40 million.

So given those odds, how confident are you that driver A will escape the year without a wreck? Now, let's add some posterior conditions.

What would you say the chances are if you know driver A is a nineteen-year-old male who drives several hours a day? Does your confidence increase or decrease if you also know he drinks and drives? Because each of the factors increases the chances of a wreck, our confidence in a crumpling outcome increases. If the posterior probabilities were uncorrelated, say the driver in question is from Scotland originally (but counted among American licensed drivers) or that he is balding prematurely, then the posterior probabilities should have no effect on our confidence about the prior probability. It is important to realize that the power of our estimation of risk comes from how much we know and how confident we are in the contributions each piece of information makes to the likelihood of a specific outcome.

The probability of event B occurring given that event A has already occurred is typically written as P (B|A)

The general multiplication rule that we used for determining the chances of tossing five heads in a row also works for conditional probabilities:

$$P \text{ (A and B)} = P \text{ (A)} \times P \text{ (B|A)}$$

The more you know, and the more experienced you are, the more confident you can be in your estimation of the probabilities, but you need to be prepared to constantly modify your estimation of your confidence based on your estimation of the number and nature of the variables involved. Does the new information matter and, if so, how much? It may also matter if other people possess or don't possess this information. General knowledge is less advantageous than expert knowledge. Insider knowledge is even more effective but also illegal in many situations.

Rule 24: Reassess your expectations whenever new information arrives or something significant changes

You have to be careful about compounding conditional probabilities, however. If the details you are adding together aren't correlated to the outcome you are trying to predict, you will falsely persuade yourself.

Kahneman has an interesting example of compounding uncompoundable probabilities leading to a false sense of confidence.

> Linda is thirty-one, outspoken, and very bright. She majored in philosophy. As a student, she was deeply concerned with issues of discrimination and social justice, and also participated in antinuclear demonstrations. (156)

Kahneman asked his test subjects, is Linda more likely a bank teller or a feminist bank teller? Most people assume the latter based on the description. Kahneman's point here is simply that this example sets up a conflict between two types of thinking, the intuitive practice of accumulating details into a stereotype and making a judgment based on that stereotype (System 1) versus applying a simple rule of probability (System 2), that two non-correlated attributes are less likely than one. What are the chances of heads coming up twice in a row? Not .50 but .25, right?

What if Linda's description included a women's studies degree? Would that change the odds of bank teller versus feminist bank teller? Well, we might try to reason by analogies here. Does earning a doctor of dental medicine degree make you a dentist? Does earning a philosophy degree make you a philosopher? Not in the same way. What about earning a degree in women's studies? In other words, the significance of the condition is more important than the condition itself. You need to know what the implications of the details are and could be. The details alone are not enough.

If a process isn't deterministic, if A doesn't cause, stipulate, or at least very strongly correlate with B, then the presence of A does not increase the chances of B + C over just C alone.

Rule 25: The chances of two uncorrelated things happening are never greater than the change of one happening alone

Your Turn

The difference between correlation and causation is critical to making good decisions because you need to know whether an act alone will have the desired effect or if context, timing, and additional factors being present or absent will influence the outcome. The problem is that our minds like to simplify what they observe and come to conclusions more quickly than they should: we ascribe cause when correlation is correct.

1.   Make a list of events in your life that had an impact on future events. To which can you ascribe a specific cause?

Expected value

Another arithmetic equation relevant for deliberation is the idea of expected value. Whenever we need to decide the current value of something that may or may not pay off in the future, we need to take the probability of it happening into account. Let's take the case of a simple gamble. How much would you pay for a ticket to win 100 dollars with a 1/2 chance of winning (and a 50 percent chance of losing, right?)? Well, the expected value is 50 dollars.

Rule 26: Expected value = outcome × probability

So if you could buy such a ticket you should, rationally or at least arithmetically speaking, be willing to pay up to 50 dollars for it. What is the expected value of a ticket to win 700,000 dollars? Consider the powerball lottery. The odds of winning the jackpot are apparently 1 in 175,223,510 (Butler). So the expected value is 700,000/175,223,510 = 0.0399 or just less than 4 cents. And it costs 2 bucks to play. Having done the math, do you still want to play? Rationally, or at least arithmetically, you don't want to play unless you can pay a nickel for the ticket (what's a penny among friends?). And yet people who are not numerically challenged still pay 2 dollars for something worth less than 4 cents.

There was an ad years ago for the New York State lottery, the tag line for which was something like "A dollar to dream." If you think about that for a second, the logic is something like, if I spend a dollar I can imagine all the things I could do and buy if I win. Once the fantasy starts, the reality (the odds of you actually winning) disappears, and it makes "sense" to spend a buck for the (astronomically bad) chance to realize your fantasies. If you wanted to talk yourself out of buying a lottery ticket and couldn't be bothered to do the math, you might try the counterstatement: "You want to tax my dreams?" Under the heading of be careful what you wish for it might also be worth looking up what the experiences of lottery winners have been. Many are miserable because they had no idea how to make good use of all that money, and the notoriety the win gave them made them targets for deception and manipulation by all kinds of people they wouldn't have met had they not "won" the lottery.

Rule 27: Don't bet against the house

Let's say that unlike lottery players you spend some time in your planning self's home. You want to choose based on the probability of an outcome and not just on the absolute value of that outcome.

Decision: Should I do A or B?

A has consequence R, which I value at 3.

B has consequence Q, which I value at 6.

Given this weighting, I should choose B because I prefer Q by twice as much over R. But what are the probabilities of me getting the consequence Q? Let's say arbitrarily that:

R has a probability of 70%. 3 × 70% = expected value 2.1.

And what is the probability of B getting me Q?

Q has a probability of 30%. 6 × 30% = expected value 1.8.

So the expected value (the basic value factoring in probability of desired outcome) of A is 2.1 while the expected value of B is 1.8. Thus I should choose A over B—even though originally I valued B at twice as much—because A is more likely to get me something I want even though I want it less than what B would get me if only it would actually get it for me. So, I have to ask myself at this point, do I take the larger risk, stand a chance of getting nothing with a 30 percent chance of getting what I really want, or should I settle for a 70 percent chance of at least getting something I want? The math suggests the latter because the difference between 2.1 and 1.8 is just 0.3. Of course we never specified the unit of measure and 0.3 might be a huge magnitude given the right object. But numerically speaking, the difference between 2.1 and 1.8 is just 0.3.

Given that the math inclines us toward A because there's a better chance of getting what we want and the difference between what we want and what we really want is so small (0.3), the numerate ("rational") decision would seem to be A. But "rationality," in a modern context, also needs to factor some elements of the "irrational" if we are really going to have a thorough decision-making process.

Character, specifically risk tolerance and aversion, and the situation (what is the magnitude of .3 in this case. Are we talking Joys or Cancers?) need to be factored in. It's not so much a *Dirty Harry* question, do I feel lucky? It's more a question of how I will feel if I take A and get on with my life. Will I forever pine over the loss of B? Or, let's say I go with B and get nothing; will I forever pine over the missed opportunity A offered? What is the psychological impact of .3 in this case?

Curiously enough, regardless of the magnitude of point .3, from a psychological perspective, it's quite likely that in fact I will have forgotten the whole thing shortly after I decide, one way or the other, regardless of the outcome. We tend to overestimate the impact of our decisions on our future happiness at the time we are making them. Bad things don't hurt as much as we anticipate they will, and good things don't please us as much either. Our happiness, in other words, is a character trait, not a matter of circumstances, at least in the long run (see Gilbert, 2013). By saying that, I'm not saying the math doesn't matter, that all decisions are irrational, only that "rational" has a somewhat more limited value than we might accord it in common usage. We are humans (stochastic beings) not automatons (deterministic entities).

The brain is a complex organ that we are only beginning to understand. While you should do the math to the extent it is actually possible to put a numeric value on an outcome and you should also adjust the weight of that number based on the odds of the event actually happening, you still need to ask yourself about both what motivates the decision and how you will really feel later on, not how you imagine you will but how you really will. Complex thought processes are not accurately reducible to simple equations. But complexity isn't synonymous with irrationality either.

Rule 28: Don't fall in love with an algorithm

Your Turn

Expected value requires that you make a decision based on the probability of each possible outcome factored into your preference. So, the perfect outcome that has only a 10 percent chance of happening amounts to a kind of all-or-nothing proposition. Is that truly what you want, or can you settle? Imagine a situation that might have multiple outcomes and then put a numerical value on the probability of each. Then see if that helps you decide something other than what your first, intuitive, preference suggested.

Utility and marginal utility

Utility is an abstract measure (utils) of how useful something is, and marginal utility is the difference in utils between two options. If you've been lost in the desert all morning and you stumble out into a suburb where a kid is selling lemonade, you'd pay 100 dollars, if you had it, for what under normal circumstances you'd only pay 1 dollar because you are dying of thirst. The more you have of something, typically the less each subsequent acquisition of that something is worth to you. Stoics and Cynics believe that anything beyond basic human needs is vanity and that, therefore, there is no marginal utility beyond just enough to keep you alive. People who luxuriate find great utility in small differences—a Rolex is better than a Fauxlex, legality aside, even if both are equally well made because the brand name signifies power, prestige, and status, intangible differences that make all the difference for some people.

Let's say you have two job offers about which everything is equal but the pay. In such a purely hypothetical case you would likely take the higher paying job. But let's say one is in a city you've always wanted to live in while the other is in a city you'd be OK with living in. How much more would the OK city job have to pay for you to choose it? Would 10,000 dollars a year make you choose Birmingham over New York? You probably should factor in difference in cost of living, housing market, and so on. Well, ten grand goes much further in Birmingham than New York City, for sure. Would you rather be broke in NYC or comfortable in Birmingham? So the utility of ten grand all things being equal is just the money, but when you factor in different cities, the utility of ten grand changes and so how you make the decision changes. Given the cost of living in NYC and other desirable places, you'd need a job paying considerably more to make the living there preferable, unless of course the city matters more than anything else.

Psychologists argue that once you are making 140,000 dollars a year, adding to your income won't add to your happiness. The number changes depending on inflation and so on, but the basic idea is that once you've covered necessities and have a disposable income to provide for a reasonable level beyond the necessary, with a cushion in case of emergency, more money has no utility. You just pay more for everything and get only faux satisfaction out of the difference, no real marginal utility. It would be irrational, therefore, to think that someone making 1 million a year is happier than someone making 140,000 dollars. Still, the irrational is a powerful force, especially when it comes to money because prestige and power are also functions of wealth. Past a certain point, money isn't about money anymore. The unit of util changes from the numerical to the psychological.

Rule 29: Don't make decisions based on false or misleading distinctions

Your Turn

1. So, how rational are you? How much more money would you need beyond what you currently have to obtain everything you want out of life? How do you place utils on things that aren't things? Think of two things you value intrinsically, in and of themselves rather than for what they can produce or for their monetary value. Now rank them. Which is better than the other?

2. In the previous paragraph I made a 140,000 dollars assertion, but I didn't say where the number came from and I attributed it to an empty signifier, "psychologists." Where did that number come from? Who are these "psychologists" of whom I spoke? See if you can track down the number.

3. Is it possible that when it comes to money marginal utility is a more useful idea than utility? In other words, is it possible that how much you have doesn't matter as much as how much more you have than your immediate friends and acquaintances? And, if that is the case, at what point would a disparity in your favor become a burden rather than a source of pleasure?

To this point we've been talking about decisions as though they are always independent of other people's actions. Often, however, we have to make decisions in response to other people's actions, and in such cases it can help to have some rules of thumb in mind. Much of the foundational thinking about decision making in social contexts comes from game theory.

Game Theory

In the broadest possible sense, there are two forms of human interaction, competition and cooperation. Strategizing about how to beat the competition and how to join them when beating them is impossible or less profitable is what game theory is about. The most famous examples are "the prisoners' dilemma," "the traveling salesman's problem," "the ultimatum game," and "brinkmanship." Some others are how to keep your opponent guessing while serving in tennis, when to discount items you are selling, and how to work an auction. Essentially, whenever people are participating in a shared activity in which the rules are universally accepted and the objectives and outcomes are unambiguous, game theory suggests that there is a purely rational optimal move in any given game-theoretic situation.

Prisoner's dilemma

The "prisoner's dilemma" is a phrase coined by the renowned mathematician Albert W. Tucker for an idea first proposed by Merrill Meeks Flood and Melvin Dresher. The game is usually presented something like this:

Two men are apprehended at the scene of a crime and detained in separate rooms. Each is promised immunity in exchange for testifying against the other, without repercussions, personal or legal. If one defects and throws his buddy in, the defector will get off and the violated buddy will get three years. If both take the deal offered by the prosecution, if both defect, they will each get two years. If both remain silent, there is a good chance they will both go free. The selfish play would be to accuse the other and so get off, but if they both do the selfish thing, they each get two years. The honorable play, and the best outcome for both, is to remain silent. The worst outcome for each would be to suffer the other's defection while remaining steadfast. What would you do? Well, what will your partner in crime do?

While the gossipy details of what was originally conceived of as a purely mathematical problem have given it a long life in popular culture and business management literature, they aren't relevant from the perspective of game theory. As William Poundstone the author of *Prisoner's Dilemma* points out isn't about, "'playing' as usually understood. It is about conflict among rational but distrusting beings" (2011, Kindle Locations 813–814).

What really matters is the way the conceptualization of the possible outcomes—win/win, win/lose, lose/win, lose/lose—helps to transfer the idea of a sample space to human interaction, to make life available to mathematics, in other words. Given this setup, the mathematically optimal decision is for each to defect, to say the other guy did it. That way they are assured the least worst sentence regardless of what the other does. This is known in game theory as minimax (or minmax) decision. If both accused parties are "rational"—again according to game theory's definition of rational, which is being able to see the options and pick the best available regardless of what the other person does—both will defect. Remaining silent would produce the best outcome, but getting it depends on the other person doing the right thing. In game theory the assumption is always that your opponent will do what's best for him and therefore what's necessarily worst for you (distrust and cynicism are built into the definition of the game). *Quod erat demonstrandum*: take the best you can get and be done with it.

The moral of this story is that while cooperation is often preferable to competition, for various reasons—character flaws, greed, fear, ambition, distrust, selfishness, and so forth—people often fail to see the greater opportunity provided by cooperation and choose competition instead. If you can win without losing anything, then go for it. But you might want to remember that there are numerous ways of counting up loses, and "the game" as it was originally designed conveniently brackets the consequences of betraying your confederate.

For the mathematically inclined, the game dramatized by the prisoner's dilemma is interesting and solvable without any accompanying narrative. Add the narrative, however, and it quickly becomes apparent that the dilemma can't be resolved by mere mathematics even though the math is always the same. The problem is that human emotions get involved, and therefore game theory's definition of "rational" breaks down. It's not that emotion renders reason useless, only that the details of who is involved and the organizations they represent and their individual character types determine how any given person would decide in a given situation. Hardened gangsters might be likely to remain mute because they know death awaits them on the outside for snitching, while spending a few years in prison only adds to their credibility when they get out. A youthful offender, on the other hand, captured with his mentor might take the hit for the sake of his superior, and yet another might throw in with the prosecution because they are offering a way out of a life of crime. As Poundstone puts it, "The solution never came. Flood and Dresher now believe that the prisoner's dilemma will never be 'solved' and nearly all game theorists agree with them. The prisoner's dilemma remains a negative result—a demonstration of what's wrong with theory, and indeed, the world" (2011, Kindle Locations 2233–2235).

Maximin strategies

Maximin strategies are used in zero-sum games in which the players move either simultaneously or sequentially. The idea is to minimize the maximum payoff to the other player by minimizing your own loss regardless of what the other player does. The idea here is that you have greater resources than your opponent such that even were he to keep winning he couldn't or wouldn't bother staying in the game. Presumably your strategy doesn't guarantee you will lose, only that you will lose the least amount possible each time you do lose. That will also mean that when you win you won't win as much as you might have on any given turn, but your plan is to win long term. There's an investment strategy along these lines in which you put money on a wide range of very volatile stocks knowing you will lose money most of the time but calculating that the one big win will pay the others off and net a profit worth the risk.

The take away of the maximin strategy is that you should factor losses into the win column as much as wins in the loss column. If you are playing an expensive game, against an opponent who will benefit from your losses, try to lose as slowly as possible so that you can stay around long enough to win. In other words, don't bet unless you have a hand that can beat better than 80 percent of the possible hands, unless you play with the same people regularly and often enough for them to learn your ways. If your opponents discover that you won't bet unless you have a strong hand, they will choose to get out every time you get in, limiting your winnings. Whenever you play the same people frequently enough that they can anticipate what you will do, you will want to randomize your play enough that they won't know whether this is a weaker than usual hand or not. This is known in game theory as a "mixed strategy."

Rule 30: Minimize your losses (and therefore the other person's gains) as a way of maximizing your gains over time

Dominant strategy

Whatever offers you the best payoff more often than not is called your *dominant strategy*. Dominant strategy is a useful concept to ponder whenever interacting with an adversarial partner who will benefit at your expense. In any game or game-like activity, what you do is often in response to what your opponent does or doesn't do. The problem is, you don't always know what they are up to or what they will do, and they may be trying to hide their true intentions and plans from you. So you might be better off just perusing what's best for you regardless of what they do or plan. If there is such a clear path of activity, it's known as your dominant strategy. If both players employ their dominant strategy, each gets the best possible outcome and the game is said to have achieved equilibrium. In the prisoner's dilemma, the dominant strategy is for each to accuse the other.

It's worth knowing what your opponent's dominant strategy is also as well as whether or not he is knowledgeable and stable enough to employ it because if he doesn't employ his dominant strategy for any reason, you might be able to exploit the situation. Still, the fundamental concept here is to ignore your opponent and peruse your own independent interests. If the game is fair, you will maximize your return over time in this fashion. Of course, a maximum return isn't necessarily a good thing. At a card table in a professional gambling hall, your maximum return is the slowest possible loss rate. The house always wins. Not playing at all might be better than getting the best you can get; this depends on the game and your reasons for playing it. You could reframe your slowest possible loss rate as the hourly cost of playing and so perceive gaming as an entertainment cost rather than as an investment strategy (a very poor choice) or a sport (a slightly misleading choice).

Rule 31: If you have a truly dominant strategy, use it

Ultimatum

The ultimatum game is a favorite experiment in economics labs. You are given a sum of money and told to share some portion of it with another person. If they accept the offer, you both get paid. If they reject the offer, you both get nothing. You get one shot at it, so what you are offering is a take-it-or-leave-it proposition. How much do you offer? From a game theory perspective, where everyone is purely rational, and to be up any amount of money is a dominant strategy, you should take even just 1 dollar if that's what the other offers you because that's 1 dollar you didn't have before. If you knew someone was going to get 99 dollars if you would accept 1 dollar, would you take the deal? Through multiple repetitions of the game it's become apparent that if you offer too little your offer will be rejected even though the other person would be getting free money for no effort on his part. It seems we find it kind of insulting if a guy stands to get 80 dollars for giving us 20 and so we'd rather get nothing just for spite. From a psychological perspective, the game's a bit more interesting if we know he stands to gain but don't know how much, but then if it's a take-it-or-leave-it proposition, not all that interesting.

The take away here is that actions perceived as greedy or lopsided generate animosity and resistance, which keep people from accepting a clear gain. From a traditional perspective, allowing emotion to minimize gain is irrational. The dominant current thinking is that to experience emotional responses generated by social conventions and practices is to be human, not imperfectly human (irrational) or all too human, but simply human. In other words, if you ignore or deny your emotions you are failing to understand yourself fully. And thus, curiously, expecting to make a purely rational decision is a weak foundation upon which to build a decision.

Rule 32: Do unto others as you would have them do unto you

Brinkmanship

Brinkmanship is a "game" in which you set your opponent and yourself on a path of mutually assured destruction believing that he will quit (surrender) before you do. The term seems to have been derived from an article written by James Shepley called, "How Dulles [secretary of state under Eisenhower] Averted War: Three Times, New Disclosures Show, He Brought Us back from the Brink" (1956, 70–80).

At any rate, perhaps the most famous example is the game of chicken played in the movie *Rebel without a Cause* (1955), in which Jim Stark (played by James Dean) and Buzz Gunderson race cars toward a cliff. Whoever bails out first loses. Whoever stays in too long dies. Spoiler alert: Gunderson gets his leather jacket sleeve caught in the door handle and goes over the cliff.

If you are going to play chicken or engage in brinkmanship or participate in any potentially destructive game and you don't have a theory of your opponent's mind that allows you to accurately predict that you will outlast him, you need to have greater resources than your opponent. So what looks to him like the end of the road is for you just the first horizon; that way you are assured he will panic and capitulate before you even start to fidget. The alternative to having greater resources is to be more willing to lose than your opponent. In all cases, appearances matter. You need to manage your opponent's perception of you. You need most of the time to appear other than you are.

If you want to get compliance without engagement, appear unstoppable, irresistible. If you know engagement is inevitable, hide your resources and give the impression of being vulnerable in a particular area so he will attack where you want him to attack. Or appear on the verge of collapse so he will throw everything at you at once, leaving you merely tired and him exhausted. Equally important is to ensure that your opponent can back down without being or feeling humiliated. If you don't leave an honorable out, your opponent will feel compelled to stay in and you will find yourself in a mutually destructive situation. Since your goal is to win without going to war (or driving over a cliff), you need to intimidate your rival while yet making him see clearly the upside to backing down.

Rule 33: Don't escalate tensions unless you have hidden reserves

Truels

A truel is a duel with three participants: the best short-range gunman in the world, the second best, and you. The rules are these. Each person has one gun with one bullet in it and only one shot can be fired at a time (the game is sequential). You are standing close enough to each other that an expert wouldn't miss. You draw straws to see who shoots first and you "win." The question is, whom do you shoot? (The question behind the question is "What are the implications of the rules?") The answer is, shoot no one; shoot the ground or otherwise waste your shot. (Shooting into the air is unnecessarily reckless. Who knows where the bullet will land? Don't shoot yourself either—that would be counterproductive since remaining alive is what winning means in the situation of a truel.) The point here is that because you can't win, your best option is to get out of the game alive. With you now unarmed, the others can safely ignore you. At this point it doesn't matter to you what happens next. If the best shoots the second best or vice versa either is likely to kill and if that happens, the only gun still loaded is in the hand of a dead combatant. If the shooter who shoots after you happens to miss, then the last combatant can shoot either of you or walk away. If she doesn't walk away, your chances of living are still better than if you had shot at one of them in the first place. If you had killed one, your chances of getting killed by the other would be nearly 100 percent. If you had missed, then the guy you missed would probably shoot the only other armed combatant (that being his safest move), and you would be as safe as if you'd shot at the ground, but he might just shoot at you in anger or out of basic instinct even. Why take that risk? Despite the absurdity of the setup here, there is an important moral to the story.

Rule 34: Don't play if you can't win

Dollar auction

There's an interesting game developed by game theorists called the dollar auction. The rules are simple. An auctioneer offers a dollar to the highest bidder. If you bid a penny and no one else bids, you get the dollar, minus your 1-penny investment. That's a pretty sweet deal. If, however, you bid one penny and someone bids two pennies and you decide, meh, I'm out, then the other bidder wins but you also have to pay 1 penny. That's the catch. The second highest bidder has to pay what she bid even though she doesn't get anything. And this is what makes the game an interesting example of irrational decision making. If you and I were playing this game, it might dawn on both of us that unless we win, we *really* lose, which will keep us bidding up the dollar. I would certainly rather get a dollar for 90 cents than have to pay 89 cents just to watch you win that dollar (even though it's only worth 10 cents). Because people don't like throwing good money after bad—hate, in other words, to lose—they are willing to lose even more. Apparently some instances of this game have ended with people bidding more than a dollar to "win" a dollar.

The dollar auction highlights an almost universal mental defect (cognitive bias), sometimes referred to as the "sunk-cost fallacy." People hate to lose so much that they have a hard time cutting their losses and running even when that would clearly be the wiser, more "rational" choice. Hope and optimism can actually be as destructive in some situations as competitiveness can be. If you're going to fail, fail as quickly (and therefore as cheaply) as possible.

Rule 35: When failure is inevitable, fail quickly and cheaply

Tit for tat

Game theory games are about cooperation and defection and they are typically discrete events. We decide to cooperate or defect in isolation from each other and when the game is over, it's over. Never to be played again and without consequences. In real life, however, people play games repeatedly and thus what you did the last time influences how I anticipate what you will do the next time: we build our theories of mind over time based on generalizations from specific experiences. In situations in which the game is played multiple times, there's an opportunity to retaliate for defections and to reward cooperation and this opportunity raises an interesting problem. How should you react to what the other person does? You should defect if the payoff exceeds the payback and you don't have scruples against defection—all's fair in love and war. The best way to combat defecting is to make everyone feel they have an equal chance and an equal stake in the process. If cooperation is obviously more profitable than defection, then cooperation is likely to win out. If, as is often the case, there's a big payoff for defection, then defection is very likely. When people do cheat—and here I'm talking in very general terms, breaking a known code of behavior, whether legal or moral—they tend to continue cheating unless they are punished or the benefit they receive from cheating goes away.

Punishment is as important as reward for ordered communal existence. If you let people freeload or take advantage of others or shared resources then you normalize socially destructive behavior. At the same time, however, if you have a policy of punishing or rewarding on the first instance, you may fail to achieve your goal of optimizing a situation. Punishment only works if the person being punished acknowledges he did wrong and is willing to accept the authority of the person sanctioning him. If he doesn't recognize the punisher as having a right to punish and/or doesn't acknowledge or understand that he did wrong, then the punishment won't correct the behavior. Without the perception of a just punishment, the cycle of retaliation will continue indefinitely, *à la* Hatfields and McCoys, until one side is annihilated or an external force intervenes.

The same is true for rewards. If a person thinks she deserves a reward, receiving it won't reinforce the behavior because the reward will be perceived as mere payment for services rendered rather than as tribute. This is why you can get better performance out of people by offering intrinsic rather than extrinsic rewards, incidentally.

So be tolerant of initial errors (give people a chance to learn) and slow to reward early good behavior. Once you perceive a pattern, you can respond effectively as long as the other person understands what you are doing and acknowledges your right to do it.

Rule 36: Don't reward or ignore bad behavior (your own or anyone else's)

Trust

In common usage, when we say we trust someone, we mean we have faith in them; we believe without evidence or security that they will do what they say they will do. If you trust someone intuitively, you accept the absence of direct evidence as a working condition. You just "know" you can trust person X and distrust person –X.

When it comes to human interaction, trust stands in for prediction. If you can predict what someone else will do, you can trust or distrust her with relative certainty. In a zero-sum game, you can trust your opponent to do what is rationally in her best interest whenever possible, which in effect will screw you. Oddly, she becomes untrustworthy if she ever does anything for you because the rules of the game exclude cooperative behavior. In a non-zero-sum game, in situations in which you can both win some and both lose some, you can trust your opponent to do what he perceives to be in his own best interests, which means to cooperate with you when there's something in it for him and to defect when there's a better payoff in defection, assuming he is a "rational" person and not a borderline personality type or a fiend. You needn't take his behavior personally and you needn't feel betrayed if he doesn't do what you expected him to. You just need to revise your expectations based on a reappraisal of the "game," that is the rules and the payoffs of the interaction you are engaged in with him. I say this as though it's a simple matter. It's not. Life's most painful lessons teach us about the difference between trust and predictability.

Rule 37: Don't make decisions based on the actions of unpredictable people

On the other hand, maybe you should re-think the whole game metaphor. In other words, maybe you need to reframe the activity you are involved in so that you can change the script and re-write the rules.

What happens to someone who treats intimate relationships as a game? What happens to someone who thoughtlessly accepts the "one true love" fiction and people who weave these two analogies together into a seamlessly coherent "love story?" Think about it. If love is a game, then there are winners and losers, and if there's only one love and you lose it, then game over. This kind of thinking leads to murder. True enough, it also leads to some great stories. But as metaphors to live by they are an all too common example of one bad intellectual decision (mistaking metaphor for reality) logically followed by disaster.

Rule 38: Don't play at life

Learning to live with uncertainty

Certainty is overrated largely because it is far more rare than we think it is. Our System 1 brains love to feel confident, in control, and to accomplish these sensations they like to simplify decision-making situations, often reducing the stochastic to the deterministic. You just tossed heads three times in a row. What are the chances of the next toss coming up heads? Still 50/50. You can be absolutely certain and yet wrong. The purpose of rules, heuristics, is simplification. Basically, if this worked last time, it will work again, and if it does, then it will work every time from then on. In deterministic settings that are truly isomorphic, that is, settings in which the points of contact between two problems exactly match, a previous solution will work again. If, for example, you have to decide what the odds of having twin daughters are and you already know the odds of getting two heads when tossing a coin four times, then problem already solved. Isomorphism is a mathematical concept for a reason. In life outside of math we don't have isomorphisms; we have analogies and analogies don't map exactly one to one. The points of only partial contact almost always matter. Uncertainty is guaranteed.

Alpha and beta errors

Would you rather innocent people be convicted or criminals go free? Obviously, you would rather have a justice system that could never make either mistake. Unfortunately, Lady Justice's blindfold signifies more than impartiality. Mistakes happen, and part of making a good decision is about deciding what the chances of a mistake are, estimating the potential damage, and balancing that estimate with the available remedies.

Let's say you have a chance to do something, and if you succeed you get a great reward but if you fail, the consequences are disastrous. Let's say the probability of success is 70 percent. Do you do it? The more confident you are in dealing with the downside (or the more ignorant you are of the details), the more likely you are to see a 70 percent chance of succeeding as a favorable chance. If you focus exclusively on how awesome success will be, then the 30 percent chance of failure will seem insignificant to you. On the other hand, if you can readily and vividly imagine the disaster, if you just saw it happen to someone else for example, or read a description, or just somehow can see it, then you will find 30 percent too risky. How you represent the situation to yourself will influence how you perceive the numbers. Since you know this, it may help to pay close attention to how the numbers were generated.

You may long for an objective measure that can eliminate doubt about a situation, a polygraph, for example, or an fMRI scan that could accurately reveal the truth. Longing for certainty is human but expecting it is a mistake. Very few of our decisions are truly deterministic and most of our objective measures are flawed. Even DNA tests can mistake identity. All tests of any kind can provide inaccurate results. In the most general terms, an inaccurate test can mislead you into thinking things are either better than they are or worse than they are.

An alpha error is seeing a relationship where none exists, that is, a false positive. If your blood is tested to see if you have a disease and the test comes back positive, suggesting you have the disease, but subsequent analysis indicates you don't have the disease, then the test was a false positive.

A beta error is *not* seeing a relationship that *does* exist, that is, a false negative. If your blood is being tested to see if you have a disease and the test comes back negative, suggesting you do not have the disease, but subsequent analysis indicates you do in fact have the disease, then the test was a false negative.

Whenever a decision hinges on a test of some kind, you need to know not just what the results of the test were but also what the error rates of the test are. If the error rate is high, you may need to do the test over again. If a retest is impossible, then you need to discount the value of the result. If the test is usually accurate, and the place that did the test has a plausible accuracy rate, then you need to fully acknowledge the result. Even then, however, it's possible to get an accurate result that doesn't prove what you think it proves, in other words the test is accurate but imprecise. If there is a causal link between two conditions and an accurate test for the presence of one condition, then if the test is positive the condition exists, unless the test was inaccurately performed or the sample was corrupted. On the other hand, if the link is merely correlated, then the presence of one isn't proof of the other even if the test was accurate and the sample clean.

After you know what the false positive and the false negative rates are, you need to assess the potential damage of each type of error. If you think everything is fine and it isn't, is that better or worse than if you think everything is bad and it's actually fine. Relieved in the latter case and startled in the other. Obviously in the case of a destructive but curable disease, not knowing you have it is very bad. Thinking you have it when you don't will be bad too, of course, but the damage will be psychological rather than physical unless the cure is destructive. But what about cases in which the downside is contained in the knowledge of the condition, when ignorance is bliss?

From the perspective of making decisions in general, you need not only to pay attention to your current state of mind as a function of recent experiences but also to think in more abstract terms about the impact of an error if there's a significant (and you know what "significant" means) chance it will happen. As Kaiser Fung points out in *Numbers Rule Your World* (2010), decreasing the false positive rate almost certainly causes an increase in the false negative rate: the more certain the results, the less accurate the test. If you want to ensure that every wrong doer is punished, then you have to be willing to punish more innocents as well. Our technologies have yet to save us from this dilemma. Some, the polygraph for example, offer imaginary solutions—a false positive.

Eradicating inaccurate test results would be best, of course, but if that is impossible, is it better to think you are wrong when you are in fact right or to think you are right when you are actually wrong? How you answer that question in a given situation tells you how you should set up the decision system, whether to err in favor of false positives or false negatives.

Rule 39: Don't confuse certainty with accuracy

Evidence

It's helpful to be well informed whenever you have to make a decision, but often becoming informed takes more time than a handful of Google searches and a few sessions comparing notes with friends. The deeper your knowledge about a range of things, and the tighter the fit between that range and your event horizons, the better you will be able to see the interconnections of various decisions. So even if you don't do research for a living, you should make a point of systematic inquiry into whatever interests you and learn to find a few new interests when something even vaguely strikes you as worth looking at. For focused research, you need a tool kit for analyzing the legitimacy of what you come across.

Consider the source of any information you get, not just do you like the person or do you trust him, but does he have reason to speak the truth or access to the relevant information, and does he have ulterior motives that might matter. (A person can be motivated by something other than the will to speak the truth and nevertheless speak the truth.) When it comes to written testimony, websites, and white papers, you also need to consider the source. A national organization focused on serving a special interest may be biased in its reporting, although it might not be as well; you need to cross-check information by finding out if others have reported similar findings. (The same findings being presented repeatedly may be just the result of cutting and pasting from blogs and websites—there's a lot of piggybacking online.)

Corporations also set up think tanks and agencies to support research in aid of their business, and while some of this research may be legitimate, given the profit motive you've got to look for corroborating evidence. Government agencies pose a similar problem. Are the data they offer politically motivated (and if they are, are the data actually invalid)? Along the same lines, online reviews are often a great source of insight, but there are people who are paid to write positive reviews and others who either get off on trashing things or have some other motive for being less than fair in their disapproval—competitors, for example. If you haven't noticed that, next time you read an article online, spend a few minutes skimming the comments section. I'm almost always left wondering how so many people have so much time on their hands. I've also noticed, however, that if I read a negative review on Amazon or anyplace that has user reviews, more often than not I will not buy the product. I use negative reviews to talk myself out of buying things (I don't need the positive to talk myself into buying them). Bit of a mind hack, that.

In addition to learning how to assess the credibility of sources, you need to learn some basics about the reliability of research data. When questionnaires are involved, an important consideration is the size of the sample and how representative of either a general population or a specific population if the research is targeted. If you want to know how people will vote, gathering exit polls is likely better than polling people out grocery shopping. People leaving the polls have likely just voted—random shoppers, you don't know. Often a truly random sample offers the best data, but getting truly random participants is difficult given that most researchers don't have access to everybody.

Whatever method provides access often influences in some way what the sample contains. A lot of psychological studies, for example, are based on the responses of undergraduate psychology majors from research universities. Think about the population that comprises the undergraduates at research universities. Not exactly representative of the world, are they? If you use a robodialer to call people to interview, your sample will be limited to people with landlines and you will exclude all of those who've gone entirely mobile.

Population size influences the size of the sample you need to get reliable data. If you have 1,000 people whose opinion you need to survey, then you need to get at least 525 responses to get a margin of error rating of ±3 percent (the pros call this the confidence interval). A margin of error of ±3 means that if you had a population of 1,000 people and 25 percent answered yes to a question, then you can be confident that had you asked the entire population, somewhere between 22 percent and 28 percent is the number answering yes to that question.

You only need 100 responses if you can make do with a reliability of ±10 percent. When you are reviewing other people's data generated from a survey, look at the size of the target population, the size of the sample, the way the sample was acquired, and the purported error rate. Generally speaking, the larger the sample size (often referred to as the N), the more meaningful the data, as long as the method of selection was legitimate: 100,000 members of the NRA (National Rifle Association) won't give you a fair indication of American attitudes toward guns; 100,000 chosen truly at random would give you a much better indication.

Because this brief book isn't about research, one other basic piece of information about research will need to suffice. Pay attention to the base rate of a population before making a decision about the validity of an observation. A classic example follows: John is six feet five inches tall. Is he more likely a doctor or a professional basketball player? Well, there are 878,194 licensed physicians in the United States (Young et al.). How many pro basketballers are there? Well, there are 30 teams with 12 per team, so there are 360 or thereabout. (We won't bother trying to figure out how many college ballers are getting paid, but you should always keep in mind that what is reported and what is real frequently aren't the same thing.) So given some person about whom you know nothing other than his height, he's much more likely one in a million than 1 in 360, right? Another common example is this: if you are one in a million in China, there are 1,300 others just like you.

As a general rule, when you seek evidence to inform a decision, make sure you don't seek only support for the position toward which you incline. This is known as confirmation bias and it's the source of a great many flawed decisions. If you want to believe something, it's easy to see evidence of it in nearly anything at all, but that doesn't mean the evidence you found is reliable. In fact, if you are inclined toward believing something, you will interpret even completely ambiguous data in your favor and reject legitimate counterevidence as biased reporting or aberrational data. Oddly enough, if you change your mind about something later, the evidence in favor of your original position may well become evidence against it. Ask anyone who has ever been divorced about her ex and chances are she will tell you that what she was attracted to initially came to repulse her eventually. That transformation has to do with how the behavior is interpreted, not the behavior itself. If you think something is true, seek evidence that proves it isn't; disconfirmation, in other words, is a much better source of evidence. And as always, suspend judgment for as long as possible.

The burden of proof is a useful concept for restraining impulsive decisions and fabulous rationalizations. As we all know, in our courts a person is presumed innocent until proven guilty. The consequence of this presumption is that the prosecution has to prove its case. If they fail to do so, the accused is vindicated. Thus the prosecution has the burden of proof. When it comes to making decisions, if you place the burden of proof on each thought that occurs to you—ask what evidence you have for this belief or insight or whatever it is—then you won't let System 1 do all the deciding. You will have become reflexively skeptical. You can take this attitude too far, so you also need to consider the type of decision at hand and the available evidence. Still, placing the burden of proof in the right place is critical to making sound decisions.

Rule 40: If you think something is true, seek evidence to the contrary

Rating systems and decision making

Numbers can be very powerful because they can be used to make very succinct arguments. Buy this wine; it's rated ninety. But what does ninety mean? And how was it derived? Is ninety significantly better than eighty-nine or worse than ninety-one? You also have to ask yourself, was this wine truly a spot-on ninety or was it eighty-nine rounded up, or eighty-three rounded up? More importantly, if the number is an average rating, how many people contributed a number to the average and what were their credentials and what were the circumstances of the measuring moment? Were they all drinking from the same bottle? How consistent is the taste from bottle to bottle? Even yet more important than questioning the reliability of the number is questioning its relevance. When you are buying a bottle of wine, or a comic book, or a movie, or anything else with a point scale marketing strategy, are you buying the product or some statement about yourself as represented by the number? I'm the sort of person who buys a ninety bottle of wine. Or, I'm the sort of person who can distinguish a ninety from a seventy. Or are you really just interested in the effects of alcohol and prefer a grape-flavored medium? In other words, don't mistake a product for the experience of the product. Steak or sizzle?

While mistaking a product for an experience might lead to poor decisions of no consequence when buying a bottle of wine or renting a movie, it's a mistake that might matter a great deal when it comes to choosing a college or choosing to hire a 3.8 GPA (grade point average) graduate over a 3.0 GPA. The same questions apply. Not all 3.8 GPAs are equal. Did the person with that number take a tough or easy mix of classes? Tough in a general sense or tough for them? Did they stick out a steep learning curve? Is the school rigorous in its standards, and if so how rigorous and how do you know how "rigor" is measured? Do you need someone who tests well? Or do you need someone creative, innovative, and durable? These are qualities that are not often indicated by the same signs.

One last example of a problematic number: horsepower. It seems simple enough to say that a 200 horsepower car is less powerful than a 300 horsepower car, but what difference does 100 horsepower make in general and more importantly to you in particular? Car aficionados will tell you torque is a better measure of power because if the power from the engine isn't efficiently transferred to the wheels, you end up with a tire-shredding machine. How often do you drag race anyway? But torque sounds abstract and horsepower sounds concrete and meaningful even though, let's face it, most of us have never ridden a horse let alone have a real idea about what kind of power comes from harnessing several together. The image of 300 horses pulling in tandem is compelling, but the number is just stagecraft.

We can make the same arguments about GPAs and IQs and LDL and HDL numbers and, really, nearly any number you can think of. Numbers can be precise without being meaningful, and even when a number is meaningful its significance may be overstated. Just because something can be quantified doesn't mean it is thereby simply understood.

People, advertisers especially, will sometimes use a percentage rather than a number because it sounds more impressive. A recent ad for Kindle's Paperwhite, for example, argues that it is 30 percent lighter than an iPad mini. Kind of impressive, but what exactly are we talking about? The iPad weighs apparently 0.73 of a pound while the Paperwhite weighs 0.49. In grams, if that helps, you are comparing 331 grams to 222 grams. Is that a difference that makes a difference? Maybe over time, if you read for four hours at a clip. But undeniably 30 percent sounds more impressive than twenty-one tenths of an ounce. Don't just look at the numbers. Think about what they are said to represent and represent them to yourself in alternative ways.

Averages are another example of potentially problematic numbers. An outlier or two can significantly skew an average to the point at which it looks either much better or much worse than it actually is. If you use a bell curve to control for outliers, you can perhaps rationalize your sample better and get a more helpful number but at the cost of eliminating the outliers. Sometimes an outlier is critically important. "Don't cross a river that's four feet deep on average" (Taleb 2007, 3692) as Taleb explains in excruciating detail in *The Black Swan.*

You also need to consider the number of entries in the sample. I was watching an international friendly match between the American and the Belgium national soccer teams a while back (May 2013) when the commentator celebrated an American goal by saying, "That's the first time the American's have scored on the Belgians since 1930," which sounded impressive until he added, "Mind you, they've only played two or three times over the years." Eight-three years. Suddenly, not all that impressive.

Rule 41: Make certain your numbers are meaningful and not just precise

Theory versus practice

The real world and the theoretical world are often at odds. A nice example of this phenomenon has to do with the most efficient way to board a plane. An astrophysicist named Jason Steffans has developed a plane-boarding procedure that is more efficient than any currently used plan, but it takes so much prior organization on the part of fliers that it is impossible to implement (Steffen; Public Broadcasting Service 2013). This is typical of certain kinds of theory-practice trade-offs.

Rule 42: Make sure your solutions are practicable

Overconfidence

The carpenter's rule applies by analogy to deciding. People who are skeptical by nature, who doubt the validity of evidence, the plausibility of stories, the reliability of people, and their own abilities and motivations tend to be much more careful thinkers than their less ponderous true believer counterparts. Skeptics don't act unthinkingly. It is almost always better to think before you act, but if you speak skeptically in public, if you require public consensus around probabilistic conclusions, people may think you indecisive or weak or worse. People are impressed by confidence and they think that confidence manifests itself in assertions of certainty.

Unfortunately, one of the greatest sources of error is overconfidence (Hallinan 2009) because it leads us to ignore counterevidence and to underestimate risk.

So if you have to decide in public, do your thinking before the lights come up and the cameras comes on. Speak confidently and hedge your bets as surreptitiously as possible, without appearing cryptic, vague or indecisive. "We have every reason to believe" and "We are cautiously optimistic" are a couple of common clichés that take this stance.

One of the questions we ask ourselves when trying to make up our minds is how will I feel if I take (or don't take) this job, marry this person, win this bet, or whatever it is. The problem with this question, as psychologists tell us, is that we are "viewing the future in a vacuum"

(Wilson 2004, 157) when we ask it. Just as we can't usefully compare apples to oranges, we can't usefully compare now with later. The best you can do is the best you can do on any given day given what you know and what you don't know.

Rule 43: Question twice, act once

CHAPTER 3
Decision-Making Processes

Decision-Making Processes

The idea that there is an ideal or even an optimal decision-making process fails to account for the fact that there are different kinds of decisions, different contexts, and different selves, to say nothing of the two-system mind/brain. While it is true, for example, that some intuitive decisions are based on prejudicial evidence, stereotypes, or unwarranted assumptions, and thus are best restrained by some reflection and deliberation, it is also the case that turning an impulsive selection moment into a deliberative situation would render you indecisive: "Where do you want to eat dinner?" "I don't know; you pick." "No, you pick. . . ." It is tempting to think that a person who has had a great deal of success in one area in life, made a lot of money or won a lot of awards or received numerous prestigious degrees, for example, must be a very good decision maker in general. But we often hear of highly respected people making really foolish decisions.[6]

The different kinds of decision moments, unconscious, intuitive, and deliberate, require different decision-making processes. Each process should also take context into account. A spur of the moment, done-and-forgotten kind of decision can't accommodate a ponderous process, while an until-death-do-us-part decision probably would turn out better if pondered over the course of at least a few dates. What works for an individual may not work at all for a group. Your decision-making processes have to accommodate differences in time and place and setting as well as the amount of available information, the amount of missing information, and the ratio of risk to reward.

---

6. For a vivid example, check out the case of Paul Frampton and Denise Milani, the particle physicist and the Czech "model" (Swann 2011).

Not all decisions are the same; therefore, no one process will always work well. So you need several processes and you need to tailor each of them to the situation.

Rule 44: Develop decision-specific decision-making processes

An elaborated unconscious decision process

Strictly speaking, there's no way to alter an unconscious decision process because you would need to become conscious of it through reflection on a negative outcome, and that would mean turning the unconscious into the semiconscious. In most unconscious decision situations there's no need to break out of the routine or rewrite the script. It's only when our habits and inclinations are starting to bore us or are starting to cause problems, as happens with addictions to dangerous substances or unhealthy lifestyle choices, that we might want to re-write a decision script.

The difficulty is to cultivate awareness of our inclinations and thus to learn to see them not as "natural" or "right" but as born of circumstances, cultural norms, traditions, personal habits, and in some cases fossilized errors in judgment. You can learn to get up early. You can learn to skip dessert. You can learn to speak another language. If you can question your impulses you can modify your behavior. It's possible, perhaps, that the hardware can't be altered, but the software can be re-written. Bringing conscious awareness to everything you do gives you an opportunity to modify things you would otherwise either fail to notice or defend mindlessly as the right thing to do. The downside of becoming constantly conscious is that you will spend time pondering perhaps trivial options and you may derail your trains of thought from time to time. Do I really love to read or am I actually hiding from my current circumstances? Do I love playing first person shooter video games because they are fun or are they fun because I'm frustrated by my current circumstances? Am I hungry or anxious?

Questioning your preferences is a good idea because doing so makes you more self aware. At the same time, however, you can't permanently disable autopilot and continue functioning. If every decision were entirely conscious you would do very little and be constantly exhausted. Some decisions need to be made unconsciously. You can't drive a car or ride a bicycle consciously, for example. Once you learn how it's done, you just do it from then on without thinking about how you do it. There's a concept called "ego depletion" that suggests that whenever you have to make a number of thoughtful decisions you get cognitively tired and your willpower drops off. If you ever had a stressful day and found yourself wrecking your diet plans by eating ice cream from the container in the evening, you may have been suffering from ego depletion. Cognitive resources are finite and you have to distribute them effectively.

Here's a tool for making some decisions in advance of their arrival to reduce the number of times you need to make essentially the same decision and thus as a way of conserving cognitive energy and maintaining focus.

The Eisenhower decision matrix (EDM) is a simple idea popularized by Stephen Covey in his book *The Seven Habits of Highly Effective People* (1989). The decision matrix is a graphic organizer to help you prioritize the events that fill your days. By placing each item you encounter or might encounter daily into the appropriate box, you decide in advance how to deal with it. Making decisions in advance can be powerfully liberating. A simple example follows: when trying to write, turn off your email (and your Twitter and Snapchat and Facebook alerts). Instead of getting continually distracted by having to decide whether or not a given ding! matters, and then cumulatively spending time getting back into what you were doing after each distraction, you can decide once now to decide about all of them later.

The EDM starts with a basic distinction between urgent and important. The difference between urgent and important is time. Just because something is urgent doesn't mean it is also important. And just because something is important doesn't mean it needs your immediate attention.

The Eisenhower decision matrix

	Urgent	Not urgent
Important	Building on fire, deadlines, bills, illness, real crisis	Education, employment, family, arts, crafts, hobbies, exercise, health
Unimportant	Email, calls, sales pitches, constantly needy people, side projects	Social networking, television, video games

You may not agree with where I placed the items in the boxes. That's fine. It's the boxes that are important. When your turn comes in a moment, fill out the boxes for yourself.

Anything burning (urgent/important) needs immediate attention and focus—kill autopilot and pay attention.

Anything important but not urgent needs regular attention and constant care. These are your long-term, in some cases lifelong, goals, the activities you value above all else. You can't neglect these items for long. But you can't focus on them exclusively because there are other things in your life, and, anyway, they will take a long time to complete and some will always be work in progress. To ensure that the important nonurgent parts of your life get the constant attention they need, you can set up a schedule that more or less puts looking after them on a kind of autopilot, not mindless certainly, but routinely built into the vast majority of your days. When it comes to exercise, for example, your health requires a bit of that every day. So you could join a gym. But you could also, perhaps, choose to live close enough to work to walk or ride a bike. Decision made once, problem solved once and forever.

Anything that is urgent insists on being dealt with immediately, but if it isn't also important, you might delegate it to someone else or put it off until a preset finite time.

Anything unimportant and not urgent should be actively ignored. At the very least you should keep these items *off* autopilot to avoid pointless and potentially unhealthy obsessions and even addictions.

Your Turn
Build an EDM and fill in the blanks.

A simple deterministic decision process—the pros and cons list

The simplest decision-making procedure takes a single issue—should I or should I not buy this house—and then lists the arguments for and the arguments against, weighting each argument as the value becomes apparent. Benjamin Franklin famously advocated this practice in a letter to Joseph Priestly in the fall of 1772.

> My Way is, to divide half a Sheet of Paper by a Line into two Columns, writing over the one Pro, and over the other Con.

Then during three or four Days Consideration I put down under the different Heads short Hints of the different Motives that at different Times occur to me for or against the Measure. When I have thus got them all together in one View, I endeavour to estimate their respective Weights; and where I find two, one on each side, that seem equal, I strike them both out: If I find a Reason pro equal to some two Reasons con, I strike out the three. If I judge some two Reasons con equal to some three Reasons pro, I strike out the five; and thus proceeding I find at length where the Ballance lies; and if after a Day or two of farther Consideration nothing new that is of Importance occurs on either side, I come to a Determination accordingly.

And tho' the Weight of Reasons cannot be taken with the Precision of Algebraic Quantities, yet when each is thus considered separately and comparatively, and the whole lies before me, I think I can judge better, and am less likely to take a rash Step; and in fact I have found great Advantage from this kind of Equation, in what may be called Moral or Prudential Algebra. (*Mr. Franklin: A Selection from His Personal Letters.* Contributors: Whitfield J. Bell, Jr., editor, Franklin, author, Leonard W. Labaree, editor. Publisher: Yale University Press: New Haven, CT 1956. http://www.procon.org/view.background-resource.php?resourceID=1474 accessed September 2014)

While most of us have come across the idea of a pros and cons list, what's especially interesting about Franklin's explanation of the practice is the idea that one should take "three or four Days Consideration" to do it. Time allows us to make sure that we aren't in the grip of a temporary mood or otherwise motivated by something ephemeral. Time, essentially, allows us to use reflection as a way to shift from intuition to deliberation, which for some decisions will enable better outcomes.

If you had trouble following Franklin's eighteenth-century prose, here is what his practice might look like in modern tabular form. The unit of measure, the weight, is an arbitrary scale, from 1 to 10, 10 being essential. Anything that didn't get at least a 1 shouldn't be on the list at all. Anything that gets a 10 ends the discussion, so if there's an item on the con side that gets a 10, the house is a no-go. Similarly, a 10 on the pro side makes the decision for the affirmative. In effect, no single attribute should be the decisive factor and thus there shouldn't be any 10s. Why? Because refusing to accept the idea of perfect makes you think more carefully about the value of things. Perfect is a cop-out, the indulgence of a preference, not a decision, and certainly not a deliberate process.

Should we buy this house?

Pro	Weight	Con	Weight	Dif.
Great school district	8	Big commute	6	2
Right number of rooms for now	7	Maxed out budget, no room for additions	2	5
Big yard	6	Yard work	7	1
New construction, new systems	8	Will need blinds, fans, landscaping	8	0
Big box stores nearby	4	No boutiques	3	1
Convenient grocery chains	4	No farmer's market	5	−1
Great playground, bike paths, nature trails	8	Drive everywhere, even to playground	6	2
Many national chain restaurants	3	No locally owned and operated eateries	7	−4
Total	48		44	4

Although Franklin doesn't mention using numbers, placing a numerical value next to each criterion, adding the total, and then subtracting the larger from the smaller to find the difference can accomplish his balancing method. The difference then offers a magnitude of preferences. Even if your numbers aren't actual units of measure but really just subjective judgments about the importance of a criterion, you will still learn something about what you want.

The pros and cons list can be effective for rationalizing or justifying a decision to do or not do some one thing, but it gets much more complicated if there are multiple alternatives. Once it's no longer a question of should I buy this house or not but rather should I buy this house or this other house or maybe rent this third house, the balancing part of the process becomes much more difficult. You can clarify complicated decision moments by first reducing them to a single issue, by first deciding whether to rent or buy, for example, and then using the pros and cons technique to deliberately choose one option over another.

If you know you have a positive inclination in one direction, lean hard in the other direction. The list of why you should do what your inclination leans you toward will come quickly and automatically, the effect of the confirmation bias that leads us to see in practically everything evidence supporting our inclinations. It's a sad realization perhaps, but you need to learn how to rain on your own parade if you want to think deliberately. If you want to do something, pay careful attention to the cons side of the equation. If you don't want to do something, pay more careful attention to the pros side. Figuring out in advance what an opposing voice might say will also better prepare you to justify a decision if you have to.

Rule 45: Play the Devil's advocate

A model for training intuitive decision-making processes

If you want to learn how to do something that requires rapid execution of sequenced decisions made with little conscious intervention—for example, writing prose or code; using a complex computer program like Photoshop; learning to speak a foreign language; learning how to play a musical instrument; learning a sport; or learning a complex game like Chess or Go—then all you need is information, projects to practice on, and seat time. Given these, you will train your intuitive responses and become automatic in that decision setting. Whether or not you will get good at whatever it is depends on how much seat time and how deliberate your practice is, as well as how physically and cognitively suited to the task you are, but you will certainly learn how to do it and will almost certainly get better over time. You might plateau. You might never win a prize, but you can certainly get much better than you were when you first started. As the slope of your improvement levels off, you will either decrease your efforts and content yourself with your final state or you will triple your efforts to gain even a tiny fraction of improvement. How badly do you want this?

The paradigm for training intuitive decision processes is as follows.

1.   Know your goal.

    a.   Be as specific and quantified as possible, for example, not just learn French but be able to order a meal in French and carry on a brief conversation with the waiter, or be able to read *Le Monde*.

2. Determine the steps involved.

    a. Break the activity into parts.

    b. Practice each part slowly and deliberately.

    c. Seek immediate feedback (coach, fellow learner, both).

3. Put the steps together into a single performance.

    a. Practice the sequence repeatedly.

    b. Seek immediate feedback.

    c. Debrief.

    d. Keep a log.

4. Repeat step 3 obsessively until the performance becomes unconscious.

5. Seek a community of practitioners if you aren't already a member of one.

For more on intuitive decision making, see Gary Klein (1999). For more on developing expertise, see Ericssen (2009).

At some point, having become relatively good at whatever you set out to learn, you will likely have to decide whether to push on to greater heights, subordinating other goals to this one goal, or accept the plateau and find other goals. At that point you will need to figure out how your goals interrelate, which ones reinforce each other and which ones conflict. Anything you spend a lot of time on will become linked to other decisions, so you might want to take that into account as well.

An elaborated stochastic decision process

1. What is your goal?

    a. Remember to clarify it if it's in any way indistinct.

2. Is this your decision alone, are others affected, should they be consulted?

    a. Are there other people directly or indirectly involved?

    b. If the outcome depends on the efforts of other people, then you have to factor their reliability and therefore their character and motivation into the possible outcomes. The more people involved, the more ways things can go other than planned.

    c.   Do you have competitors who might interfere with your plans or somehow alter the landscape? Is this in any way a zero-sum "game," and if it is can it be transformed somehow into a win-win?

    d.   Do you have allies or colleagues who will help?

3.   Do you have time to do research, reflect on previous decisions, ask others?

    a.   Are you truly in a hurry, or are you being impatient or even impulsive? Are you being pressured by someone else?

    b.   If you don't have time to deliberate, then ask yourself if this situation is similar to past ones, isomorphic, analogous, merely reminiscent, or actually different. If it is different, will the difference matter?

    c.   If it's isomorphic or at least analogous, then you can perhaps rely on your past experience to inform your current decision.

    d.   If you go with your inclinations will you have to justify the decision later?

    e.   If you will have to justify the decision, then you may want to delay long enough to know what you will say if questioned.

4.   What kind of deliberative moment is this?

    a.   Is this a one-timer?

    b.   Does it have long-term or short-term consequences or some mixture of both?

    c.   Is there a chance it will become a habit or otherwise have unintended consequences?

    d.   Are there changes on the horizon?

    e.   Is this decision linked to others decisions?

5.   Is this a stochastic decision-making process?

    a.   How many variables are there?

    b.   Of the variables, how many are dependent, partially dependent, interdependent?

    c.   What degree of control do you have over each of these variables?

6.   What are the possible outcomes (the sample space)?

A common error in deliberative thinking is taking too narrow a view of a situation, seeing only the win-lose instead of also seeing the win-win, for example, or being too tightly focused on the here and now and not paying attention to what might happen next. People also often allow others to frame their options to disadvantage, being talked into thinking that time is running out, for example, or that an opportunity is unique or rare when it isn't really, or that an opportunity is a threat. When deliberating about anything, you need to work hard at figuring out what ALL of the possible outcomes are. Know the sample space.

Know your sample space. The typical patterns of options are as follows:

1.   A or nothing (no real or even apparent options, dilemmas, ultimatums, incomparable alternatives, but also impulses and mindless reflexes).

2.   A or B (the basic decision situation). If you can't decide between one or the other, flip a coin. If you don't like the result, you need to recognize that you do in fact have a preference.

3.   A and B (an optional alternative to the basic pattern often missed by impatient or conventional thinkers or restrained by thoughts about greed, fair play, or other forms of conventional morality. There's nothing wrong with that, only in allowing conventions to blind you to possibilities. A person who chooses to do the right thing is superior to the person who fails to notice the wrong thing to do. As a deliberative thinker, your goal is to see every possibility).

4.   Neither A nor B (refusing to participate is almost always an option, although people often fail to notice the option because they are afraid they will miss out on something).

5.   Some A and some B (substitutions and amalgamations are often possible).

Wait before deciding (delay, wait for new or better information, for something else to happen, for someone else to move). And sometimes the options will have variations such as A^1 and B^2.

How do you know which pattern applies in a given situation? You have to think each deliberative situation through and you need to be wary of people trying to limit your possibilities to just one of these options. You also need to make sure you aren't limiting your perception of the options. Most of the time they are all possible, but our inclination to remain in System 1 ways of thinking may keep us from seeing the less obvious, less conventional possibilities.

People who write about negotiation often point out that in the short term, when a negotiation will happen just once and never again, an aggressive, zero-sum, I win you lose stance, can work in our favor. In other words, A *or* B is a reasonable frame short term. But long term, because I win you lose creates animosity, distrust, and bad feelings generally, not to mention a ripple of bad reputation, being able to find the A *and* B, the win-win, is preferable because if we can all get what we want and need, we succeed with our reputations intact.

When you go house hunting, for example, you might find the perfect house that is 20 percent over your budget and completely unrealistic and then find one that's not quite what you want but has potential and is only 5 percent over your budget. It's still over budget and you should keep looking, but 15 percent less over budget looks better by contrast than it should in an absolute sense. In this case, *neither* A *nor* B is the better decision, but the frame of reference makes that option harder to see.

There's a variation on the A *or* B choice model that is sometimes employed by salespeople and people looking to close a deal in general. It's predicated on the observation that when faced with an *either* A *or* B scenario, in which A and B are hard to compare because they are very different, you can get a person to commit to one by also presenting a mildly inferior version of, say, the B option. Thus the choice on offer is A *or* B *or* –B. When presented with this model of options, according to Dan Ariely (2008, 10), people will tend to opt for B. While A or B presents a kind of dilemma because they are so different, the obviously simple comparison of B to –B makes people abandon the A option to focus instead on the simpler question, B or –B, and thus quickly conclude B is preferable to either –B *or* A. Ariely calls this tactic "the decoy" and you've probably seen it when shopping for a product that is sold by levels, like gold, silver, or platinum, where one option isn't really desirable but it surreptitiously makes one of the other two seem preferable. Thus your preference is guided to the company's preference like a magician draws your eye to the middle card in a fan, while you're left thinking you made a "free" choice. Ariely also points to another variation on the illusion of choice when he observes, "Most transactions have an upside and a downside, but when something is FREE! we forget the downside" (60). Consumers, in other words, and we are all consumers, are easily distracted by bogus options—the *premium* as it is called. What follows the "BUT WAIT THERE'S MORE" keeps us from focusing with knitted brow on the true choice. Do I want this or not? becomes, oh, I get two for one or one free or buy one get one free. These are all the same distraction technique. Free trials, try before you buy, and free introductory offers offer illusory choices. There's no such thing as free checking just as there's no such thing as a free lunch. You will pay if you play.

Your options never include only what's being presented by someone trying to guide a decision, but neither do they exclusively include only the options you think you see. Even an A *or* B option is also always a *neither* A *nor* B. You can opt out of deciding and you can stall if you can't opt out.

1. What is the probability of each outcome?

   a. Divide the sample space by the desire outcome.

2. Are there any conditional probabilities?

   a. List each condition.

   b. Estimate how each condition alters your level of confidence in the outcome.

3. What is the expected value of each outcome?

4. What is the expected utility of each outcome?

5. What are the risks, the probability of each, the cost of each, and the remedies?

   a. You will need to balance the magnitude of a risk against the probability of its happening, not the probability of it's not happening. Focused as you are on your goal, you may be inclined to neglect the risk side of your deliberations and so be unprepared to deal with them if they happen. Optimism is a cognitive bias.

6. What are the contingencies, the Plans B and C, but also the work-arounds for complications encountered along the way?

   a. If there is no Plan B, how will you deal with the negative results? What resources do you have, financial, social, and emotional?

7. If you achieve your goal, what's next?

For really long-term decisions, it will likely be helpful to separate the deliberations from the execution, in other words, the thinking from the doing.

Once you've decided to kill autopilot and fully articulate your intuition, that is, once you've decided to go full-on deliberative, you need to be as specific and precise as possible in as many matters as possible. Let's say you think you want to open a restaurant. You've got a killer barbecue skill set and a restaurant downtown just went under. You've got a dream, but can you realize it?

You'll need to know what the rent is, of course, and the upkeep. How old is the equipment? What do gas, electricity, water, and waste removal cost? What is the parking capacity? What are the taxes? What will the tableware for each table cost? What are the costs of labor and health insurance, but also how do you hire reliable people and how do you make sure they work at optimal capacity? You also need to know the cost of the food down to the plate. What food alternatives are available at different seasons in the year, what should you sub out permanently if the price of something goes up, and what can you switch to if that price goes down? What is the profit margin on each dish? How many plates a day do you have to sell every day to make a go of it? How many seats do you have and what does each seat need to make each day of the week? How long will it be before you turn a profit?

You also need to know concrete details about the context of your decision. Why is the restaurant space you are looking at now available? Did it go under because of some mistake the previous proprietor made, or did they retire after years of good business? Were there problems with the neighbors? Given the optimism bias we all labor under, what is the general rate of failure for new restaurants in your area? And what is your personal record? And much as you like to barbecue, what would it be like to get up at three every morning to start the fires and stand next to a smoking pit twelve hours a day? What other reality checks can you think of?

You need, in other words, the concrete and specific details of every dollar in and every dollar out but also what your day to day would be like. If you are going to make successful decisions, you need to practice turning daydreams into deliberations, and that means focusing always on concrete and specific details.

Rule 46: Turn your daydreams into deliberations by focusing on every detail

Who are you?

It's ancient advice to know yourself, of course. But what does it mean? Who are you really? And which of the three selves are you currently being? Knowing your self is a life's work. Knowing your decision style default and learning how to modify it based on analysis of the decision situation at hand is a critical step in the process of improving your decision processes. Another important way to get a grip on how you influence your own decisions is to become familiar with the common cognitive biases and to figure out which ones you are most prone to in what circumstances and what you might do, either systemically or cognitively, to keep them from deluding you. Although you can't turn the biases off, and some of them in some settings may actually be helpful heuristics in the positive sense of a potentially useful cognitive shortcut for deciding quickly, they are also capable of producing systematic errors.

Below is a list of the most common cognitive biases and a brief definition. I've offered elaboration of most of them throughout this book, but having a checklist separate from the rest of the advice might be helpful. Rank them in order of significance to you and make a note to yourself about why you think each deserves the place you put it in. Whenever you have a decision to make, review the list and ask yourself which ones might be in play.

The cognitive biases

- Above average effect—thinking you're smarter, less biased, better looking, better read, just generally all round better than everyone else. It's more than a little difficult to identify with this quirk of mind. But keep a list of the number of times you mutter "idiot" about someone during any given day, and then revisit the above average effect.

- Ambiguity effect—mistaking ignorance for complexity. If you are thinking about something for the first time, you may think it is very complex and you might be right. But someone with more experience might see more clearly how simple it is. What looks stochastic to a novice might look deterministic to an expert. However, the opposite is also true, and people who are in a hurry or are impatient by nature (or feeling pressured or frightened) may try to simplify when they shouldn't.

- Anchoring effect—focusing too tightly on a single option or piece of information. When it comes to deciding, anchoring can be a killer because it limits our interpretation of the sample space and thus limits our perception of our options. Before you ask yourself, "How will this turn out?" ask yourself "What are *all* of the ways this might turn out?"

- Attentional bias—seeing only what you are focusing on and not what's happening around what you are focused on. Look up "the invisible gorilla" the next time you're on YouTube.

- Availability heuristic—seizing on a recent or memorable event as proof of something or thinking that something isn't likely because you have no experience of it, basically using your own experience as a general frame of reference.

- Bandwagon—following the crowd, thinking what others are doing is normal or that what is normal is right.

- Base rate error—focusing on irrelevant details and ignoring general probability when trying to determine a specific probability. If a pill cures headaches within two hours in one patient in ten, is it an effective headache medication? Well, how many headaches go away in two hours when no pill of any kind is taken? And how many when a placebo is taken?

- Confirmation bias—emphasizing evidence for a preferred belief and discounting or entirely missing counterevidence. There is a related effect on memory. We are much more likely to remember evidence that fits our existing beliefs and forget anything that contradicts them.

- Contrast effect—overvaluing something because it is among inferior examples or undervaluing something because it is among superior examples.

- Endowment effect—overvaluing your possessions and attributes while undervaluing those of others. When it comes to our personal possessions, fair market value often leaves us cold.

- Framing effect—seeing only a piece of the picture, missing important details as a result of tunnel vision or just narrow focusing. Pull back, metaphorically speaking. Learn to see a threat as a challenge, a lose-win as a win-win, a complaint as an opportunity, a loss of one kind as a gain of another.

- Frequency effect—thinking that something has become popular recently when in fact it has always been popular and you've only just started noticing it. Like all of the cognitive biases, essentially mistaking a subjective phenomenon for an objective one.

- Gambler's fallacy—thinking that a future event will be influenced by a past event. If I rolled snake eyes last time, there's no way I'm going to roll it this time (actually, the chance of snake eyes is always one in thirty-six, no matter what you rolled last time).

- Hindsight bias—seeing a probabilistic event (might or might not have happened) as inevitable after it happened and deriding others for not seeing it coming or deluding yourself into thinking you knew it all along. We live life forward but make sense of if backward, as Soren Kierkegaard said.

- Hot hand fallacy—thinking success leads to greater chance of success (the opposite of jinx) in situations in which confidence isn't the sole factor. From a statistical perspective, while people can improve incrementally over time, if you look at performance data over the long haul, you won't find real runs (or slumps), just aberrations that regress to the mean. A good day is just a good day. And a bad day is just a bad day. Don't confuse a run with a trend.

- Illusion of control—believing you have greater influence over an outcome than you actually have. Chance, other factors, other people, or all three may have more impact than you realize when you are under the illusion of control. You needn't just let go and let God in such cases, but you might want to unclench your fists.

- Illusion of coherence—mistaking coherence for validity. Just because something makes sense doesn't mean it's true. The more vivid a description, the more compelling it is, but a description is just a description. Descriptions aren't evidence. We use details to identify features but details can be simulated, faked, or even just imagined, with the result that we make inferential mistakes. If something matches a defective mental model, the match is all we notice. Indeed, the defects in the model are thereby made even less visible.

- Loss aversion—failing to take a reasonable risk out of fear of losing something of lesser value that you nevertheless already have. Most people feel the loss of 5 dollars more keenly than the win of 10 dollars and so won't take a reasonable chance to make 10 dollars. What's a "reasonable" chance? Well, if you were playing with the house's money it would be much greater than if you were playing with your own money.

- Magical thinking—mistaking coincidence for cause or seeing a causal connection between two independent events. Magical thinking is a natural result of our mind's desire to create coherence and find meaning. We can't help seeing patterns and making connections even when they don't exist because meaninglessness and chaos make us very uncomfortable. A specific version of this bias is mistaking correlation for causation, assuming that one event causes another because as one changes, the other does as well. Magical thinking plays a significant part in the illusions of coherence and control. If you ever thought you could will your team to win or felt guilty because you wished disappointment on someone who then suffered a disappointment, you were thinking magically.

- Mere exposure effect—preferring something merely because it is familiar, a regular part of your existence, or a feature little noticed but nonthreatening and therefore acceptable. The opposite is xenophobia, fear of the unfamiliar. If this rates high on your list, you might want to try embracing the devil you don't know.

- Naïve realism—believing the world is exactly as you see it, that your perceptions are accurate and complete, your thoughts logical, your actions rational or at least justifiable, and your memory like a video-recording device. If you want to make good decisions in complex settings, you have to eliminate this bias.

- Normalcy bias—failing to plan for a probable disaster or failure to act when it happens, freezing, the opposite of panic but with quite likely the same negative consequences. People tend to just keep going about their business even as the walls are crumbling around them.

- Optimism bias—underestimating how long something will take, or how much it will cost, and overestimating its chances of success.

- Recency illusion—allowing recent experience to unduly influence your thinking about something, thinking, for example, right after a school shooting that school shootings are becoming more frequent whereas, in fact, the frequency of such tragic and horrific events hasn't changed over the years. Basically if you think whatever is happening now will continue to happen you're living in a recency bubble.

- Self-serving bias—believing that when you are right it's because of your hard work and innate talent and when you are wrong it's because of a corrupt system, bad luck, or some other fault outside your control. If you take sole responsibility for your successes and none for your failures, you protect your ego at the expense of your improvement.

- Zero-sum bias—having a tendency to see all interaction as winner take all, failing to see opportunities for cooperation or having an inclination to reduce cooperative settings to competitive ones. Just how Machiavellian are you?

Your Turn

1. Rank the biases according to which ones you think have the greatest impact on your decisions generally.

2. Are there any you think you don't encounter?

3. Are there any you think you might overcome?

4. Which ones have you noticed others suffering from?

5. Compare notes with somebody else. Does she agree with your self-assessment? Do you agree with hers?

Motivation

If you don't know what's motivating a choice, then you aren't making a truly deliberate decision. Given the right circumstances, an intuitive approach is preferable to a deliberate one. Nevertheless, deliberate thinkers understand, or at least can explain, what is motivating their inclinations and preferences. Character traits can be key motivators.

Take for example competitive spirit (or social dominance). Some people just need to win and thus they will decide on the course of action most likely to produce victory without consideration for the nature of the "prize," which in such cases is a decision that might stand long after the competitor has moved on. Conversely, people who have a powerful urge to cooperate might decide to do what everyone else is doing without due consideration of their unique position or needs or awareness of errors the group is generally unaware of. While most people have a propensity in one direction or the other, we all have both conditions. You need to be aware of those moments when you are going with the pack and when you want to lead the way.

Similarly, if you have a conscientious nature, that is, if you feel compelled to follow through on every decision, to check off every item on your to do list, then you have to consider this character trait when making a decision. You might decide to do something you aren't entirely committed to and then be stuck, essentially, with having to force yourself through with it. Perhaps even worse, you will decide not to try something merely because you aren't sure you can finish or accomplish it. If, on the other hand, you are not a highly conscientious person, you might make decisions too lightly, a habit that will make other people doubt your resolve or your honesty but one that will certainly fill your closets with very slightly used sports equipment and hobby paraphernalia, to say nothing of wasteful monthly membership dues.

If you are open to experience, you are by character a primarily intuitive thinker. This doesn't mean that you can't deliberate effectively or, conversely, that deliberate thinkers are closed off from new experiences. It's just that if you are inclined to think through every decision thoroughly, you are likely to live a more straight line kind of life because you will be less open, less attracted to whim and random opportunities. If you find yourself always gravitating toward novel experiences, you might want to ask yourself if it's truly time for something new or if there's perhaps unfinished business that's motivating you to move on. If you are a highly deliberate thinker, you might want to push yourself from time to time to look around a bit, to ask yourself if you are truly on course or just ignoring or avoiding a valuable alternative for the sake of remaining always in character.

If you are inclined not to do something, you should ask yourself, "Am I avoiding a mistake here or making one because I'm trying to avoid the unpleasant feelings the uncertainty of the outcome is generating?" In such cases, if you can quantify the uncertainty, turn it into a risk with numerical probabilities attached, you might be able to see your way to a bolder decision and thus increase your payoffs, especially over time. You will also increase your loses occasionally: trade-offs are inevitable.

If your disinclination is motivated by fear of a loss you need to ask yourself what the real odds of losing are, if it's possible to quantify them, but you also need to question your fear. Sometimes we miss out on something better because we want to hang on to what we have and can't figure out how to have both. In decision situations that are truly either/or situations, the loss averse may cling to what they have even when they aren't happy with it because they are afraid of ending up with nothing. People who are deeply loss averse may shrink their sample space, unnecessarily limit their options as a way of avoiding unpleasant feelings, and thus over time actually reduce their chances of success as a side effect of trying to limit their exposure to loss. It is also prudent to consider reframing the idea of "loss" in any given situation in which you are fearing a negative outcome because loses are felt more keenly than gains. Is what you fear losing a true loss? Are you playing a game? Is this loss actually a decrease rather than a loss? Is it more like a change of direction or the opportunity for a new path? Just because you feel something deeply and keenly doesn't mean you will feel it forever.

In addition to knowing your character, your long-term motivations, you need to become adept at identifying transient states, moods created by the time of day, ambient temperature, blood sugar, hormone levels, competitive impulses, cooperative impulses, immediate events, and so on—contextual features that influence how you perceive your options and thus how you are inclined to choose.

Decisions triggered by primal feelings are almost always impulsive, but we can sometimes rationalize them into what looks like a deliberate decision. The problem with this process will only materialize if the decision remains after the feeling abates. Nothing dries quicker than tears, as Cicero said. Feelings such as affinity, affiliation, pride, greed, lust, fear, anger, prestige, power, romance, curiosity, adventure, comfort, and so on can motivate long-term decisions based on temporary emotional states. Poorly motivated decisions don't always turn out badly, of course, and sometimes an impulse can force a better way of life, but the mismatch between the temporary and the permanent is cause for reflection if nothing else.

Rule 47: Don't provide permanent solutions to temporary problems

Roles

Identity is bound up with what we think is expected of us based on the roles we play for others and ourselves: child, sibling, friend, parent, co-worker, spouse, acquaintance, and others. How we interpret and perform these roles influences what we think we should do in a given situation and what we think we should be doing on a regular basis. Some of the worst decisions people make are made on the assumption that doing what is expected of them even though it will make them unhappy will be better than disappointing others. People marry the wrong people, get the wrong degrees, follow the wrong career path, have children when they shouldn't, and make all manner of such life-altering decisions based on very weak personal understandings. You could argue that there's a cultural bias in what I just said, that I've clearly privileged autonomy over collectivism. You would be right. Sacrifice for the greater good is sometimes necessary, but I can't think of a greater mistake than making an unnecessary self-sacrifice based on mindless obedience to a role. On the other hand, I can't think of a more poignant decision than a conscious self-sacrifice out of obedience to a fully accepted and thoroughly understood role.

The Causes of Bad Decisions

In deterministic situations, a bad decision is one in which the process is flawed and thus the product is imperfect. In these situations you simply correct the process. You can make a point of constantly tweaking the process for continual improvement. If you don't know how the process worked and all you have is the flawed artifact as evidence of a flawed process, then you need to troubleshoot in order to fix the process and thus make better decisions going forward. If the last time you went boating you got a sunburn, don't go boating again or find some way to stay out of the sun while on the boat.

In stochastic decision situations, however, the badness of bad decisions is harder to track down. Bad stochastic decisions are either formally flawed, and therefore the outcome wasn't what we intended, or formally correct with the intended outcome but the consequences of that outcome were somehow undesirable. Formalists would say if you made the correct decision given the best possible data and the best possible thinking about the data and the results weren't what you intended, well that's not your fault. We have a phrase for precisely such situations: stuff happens. A pragmatist, on the other hand, might just say, "Whatever, you're fired."

Sometimes the timing of a decision will invalidate an otherwise correct, formally accurate decision. Buying a house just before the housing bubble breaks, accepting a buyout from a job just before a recession, or taking a leave of absence just before a major shakeup in the organizational structure at work are a few examples of potentially correct decisions that were doomed by circumstances beyond the decider's control.

When decision errors aren't the result of chance or uncontrollable complications or unforeseeable events, they are usually the result of a small number of causes. The chief cause is overconfidence. Our System 1 brains just love to jump to conclusions and often the conclusions are wrong. Another common cause of errors, also related to allowing System 1 free rein, is impatience, artificially created either by someone trying to pressure you into deciding or by yourself because you don't want to weigh the evidence, it being hard to do so, or because you suspect that the evidence won't support what your "heart" or your natural inclinations are urging you to do. For some people, indecision is a painful cognitive state, one even more painful than regret or mistakes, and thus doing anything at all is preferable to debating the options and calculating the probabilities.

Another common source of decision errors is bad data, which can be out-dated, misleading, biased, incomplete, irrelevant, or even overwhelming. In such cases, no matter how tight the thinking, the results are bound to be imperfect: garbage in, garbage out, as computer scientists say. If you make a mistake because you had bad data, you need to get better data next time, obviously. But you also need to make sure that the next time is indeed another instance of the same decision and not one that is merely similar. The best possible data for decision A isn't necessarily so perfect for decision 1A.

Finally, some decision errors are caused by bad influences: people whose goals are at cross-purposes with yours because they are trying to profit from you at your expense, they are in competition with you and can't succeed without you in some sense failing, or their achievement somehow requires your determinant. If you fall under bad influences, you are bound to make self-defeating decisions. This too seems rather obvious but the consequences can manifest themselves in surprising ways. Because we are social animals, we tend to make decisions consistent with decisions others in our social circle made. Fat is contagious. So is divorce. So are graduation from college and success at work. Choose your friends and acquaintances wisely.

Regrets

Not every bad decision is one you will regret, and there are some properly formed ones that will produce the desired outcome and still leave you less than satisfied. There are also some people who will do the wrong thing because they want to experience the result, either because they learn best experientially or because they need more vivid proof of something than inference alone can provide. These kinds of decisions aren't exactly bad in the sense that they aren't ill formed. The outcome was foreseen and the negative consequences predicted, and yet there was some value in doing it anyway. When I was six or seven, I distinctly remember looking at an electrical outlet and saying to myself, "If I stick this bobby pin in there I'll get a shock." I did it. And yes, wow, that really hurts. Sometimes an accurate inference from clear reasoning won't provide the kind of knowledge you need. Sometimes, some of us, at any rate, want to make mistakes. Good thing I was living in Canada and not China when I made that decision.

On the other hand, there's the concept of the affective fallacy. People systematically overestimate how badly they will feel if something bad happens and how good they will feel if something good happens. The overestimation is caused by focusing on the imagined event rather than on what day-to-day life will be like after it. If you image something horrible happening, the death of a loved one or the loss of a great job, you will predict that you will be miserable if it happens, and you likely will be at first but your life will go on and other things will happen and your present self will move on. That's not to say you won't have had a profound experience and be somewhat different, just that your character won't have changed fundamentally. Life goes on. If you are interested in this line of thinking, look up the works of Daniel Gilbert.

Perspective helps

You need ways to measure the significance of the outcome of a decision so that you can spend resources, psychic and material, in accordance with the magnitude of the decision. Frequently what seems like a burning issue today may seem trivial a few days or months from now; a year or so from now you may not even remember the decision, so much will have changed. Intensity of feeling is usually not the best unit of measure. The number and nature of the ramifications may tell you more about how important a decision is and therefore how much to spend on the deliberative process. If that number gets too big, however, to the point where you are feeling overwhelmed by it, maybe you should turn your deliberative dials down.

However, big decisions are often so complex that they aren't available to truly systematic analysis, which means that a leap of faith might be called for or even a toss of the dice.

Rule 48: Count to ten three different ways

What will this decision matter ten minutes from now? And ten days? And ten years?

CHAPTER 4

A Technique for Practicing Your Decision-Making Skills

As with most things in life, you need to practice before you play. Fortunately we make decisions all day long, so there's plenty of material to reflect on. Why am I doing this? What else might I do? Why am I waiting? Why am I being so impatient? What are my options? Am I sure these are the only ones? Is there some way to see these options from a different perspective, in a different light? I have an intuitive grasp here. Should I invoke System 2 or go on instinct? Have I seen this situation or something truly analogous with it before, or is this slightly different?

Questions like these invoke your metacognitive abilities. They make you think about how you are thinking, and that gives you a chance to review a decision before you make it. Slowing down almost always yields better results. Don't use your gut instinct as an excuse for sloppy thinking or impatient action. If you plan to live in a world where you have to make rapid decisions, then you need to develop expertise in that realm through deep practice and regular experience but also by listening carefully to the stories of your superiors and asking questions (again, see Klein 1999; Ericssen 2009).

Degrees of deliberative rigor

Not every decision requires the same amount or even the same kind of forethought. Indeed, mismatching the kind of decision with the style for deciding is a good way to create frustration at best and bad decisions quite often. Below is a scale you might use to practice matching decision type to decision style. Take a decision, any decision you can think of, and place it on the scale below.

From left to right we have a continuum of levels of deliberation—the amount of consciousness involved in a decision. Any given decision might not enable the level of deliberation normally attributed to such decisions. You might lack some relevant information in a specific situation that you would normally have, for example. Common constraints on deliberation are resources and contextual pressures that alter what can be done and thought. Basically, constraints are money, time, people, information, absent information, level of probability, motivation, and emotional state—level of engagement—and finally the revocability of the decision, the levels of undo available after you've done what you decided to do.

Near-term decisions tend to fall to the left side of the scale. Mid-term and longish- term decisions tend to fall right or at least may be improved by leaning right. However, because of the greater need for flexibility that long-term plans require, often you want to push those to the middle, to train your intuition to respond almost instinctively in their support because your values are aligned with your goals.

You can overthink a short-term decision, push an impulse toward deliberation, and end up either paralyzed or just pointlessly slowed down. You don't want rigor mortis to set in. You can underthink a deliberative decision, especially if you skip the part where you think about how you might justify the decision if you need to get others onboard or let the rationalization part happen in a sloppy way. If life after the poorly made decision is good, no harm, but if the dice land unluckily, you may have some serious explaining to do.

Your Turn

So where do you put a given decision and what process would you say best fits that level of rigor for you, given the constraints?

A Generalized Decision Template

Decision:

Goal the decision relates to:

Deadline:

Desired outcome:

Do you need targets or objectives?

If targets, what are they?

If objectives, what values are they associated with?

Method for assessing the decision (result or process or both):

What do you know (evidence); what don't you know (missing evidence):

Which of the cognitive biases might negatively influence your interpretation of the available evidence?

What are the possible outcomes—the sample space?

What is the probability of each possible outcome?

Are there any relevant changes on the horizon that will modify your level of certainty regarding each probability?

What is the expected value of each outcome?

If there's a tie, will marginal utility break it?

What are the possible consequences (positive and negative) of each outcome?

What potential unintended consequences might crop up?

To what future decisions is each outcome potentially linked?

How might this go wrong? What uncontrollable forces might intervene? And what contingencies do you have in place?

How did the decision turn out? Could the process be used again? If so, should it be modified in anyway?

Works Cited

Ariely, Dan. *Predictably Irrational: The Hidden Forces That Shape Our Decisions*. New York: HarperCollins Publishers, 2008.

Bechara, Antoine, Hanna Damasio, and Antonio R. Damasio. "Emotion, Decision Making and the Orbitofrontal Cortex." *Cerebral Cortex* 10, no. 3 (2000): 295–307.

Brand M., Recknor E. C., Grabenhorst F., and Bechara A. "Decisions under Ambiguity and Decisions under Risk: Correlations with Executive Functions and Comparisons of Two Different Gambling Tasks with Implicit and Explicit Rules." *Neuropsychology* 29, no. 1 (2007): 86–99.

Butler, Bill. Durango Bill's Applied Mathematics: Powerball Odds— How to Calculate the Odds and Probabilities for the Powerball Lottery. Accessed September 10, 2014. http://www.durangobill.com/PowerballOdds.html.

Covey, Stephen R. *The 7 Habits of Highly Effective People*. New York: Simon and Schuster, 1989.

Dutton, Kevin. *The Wisdom of Psychopaths: Lessons in Life from Saints, Spies and Serial Killers*. London: William Heinemann, 2012.

Eagleman, David. *Incognito: The Secret Lives of the Brain*. New York: Vintage Books, 2012.

Edwards, David. "Texas Cops Handcuff and Take 13-Year-Old White Girl from Black Guardians." *The Raw Story*, December 2, 2013. Accessed September 10, 2014. http://www.rawstory.com/rs/2013/12/02/texas-cops-handcuff-and-take-13-year-old-white-girl-from-black-guardians.

Ericssen, K. Anders. *Development of Professional Expertise: Toward Measurement of Expert Performance and Design of Optimal Learning Environments*. New York: Cambridge University Press, 2009.

Franklin, Benjamin. "Benjamin Franklin's 1772 Letter to Joseph Priestley." In *Mr. Franklin: A Selection from His Personal Letters*, ed. Leonard W. Labaree and Whitfield J. Bell, Jr. New Haven, CT: Yale University Press, 1956. Accessed September 10, 2014. http://www.procon.org/view.background-resource.php?resourceID=1474.

Fung, Kaiser. *Numbers Rule Your World: The Hidden Influence of Probability and Statistics on Everything You Do*. New York: McGraw-Hill, 2010.

Gigerenzer, Gerd. *Simple Heuristics That Make Us Smart*. Cambridge, Oxford University Press, 2000.

Gigerenzer, Gerd. "Smart Heuristics." In *Thinking, the New Science of Decision-Making, Problem-Solving, and Prediction*, ed. John Brockman, 39–54. New York: Harper Perennial, 2013.

Gilbert, Daniel. "Affective Forecasting...Or...The Big Wombassa: What You Think You're Going to Get, and What You Don't Get, When You Get What You Want." In *Thinking, the New Science of Decision-Making, Problem-Solving, and Prediction*, ed. John Brockman, 55–68. New York: Harper Perennial, 2013.

Gladwell, Malcolm. *Blink: The Power of Thinking without Thinking*. New York: Little, Brown and Co., 2005.

Hallinan, Joseph T., and Marc Cashman. *Why We Make Mistakes*. Westminster, MD: Books on Tape, 2009.

Kahneman, Daniel. *Thinking, Fast and Slow*. New York: Farrar, Straus and Giroux, 2013.

Klein, Gary. *Sources of Power: How People Make Decisions*. Cambridge, MA: MIT Press, 1999.

Lewis, W. H. *Why Flip a Coin: The Art and Science of Good Decisions*. Hoboken, NJ: Wiley, 1998.

Lieberman, David J. *You Can Read Anyone: Never Be Fooled, Lied To or Taken Advantage Of Again*. Prince Frederick, MD: Recorded Books, 2008.

McRaney, David. *You Are Not So Smart: Why You Have Too Many Friends on Facebook, Why Your Memory Is Mostly Fiction, and 46 Other Ways You're Deluding Yourself*. New York: Gotham Books, 2012.

Miller, George A. *Psychology: The Science of Mental Life*. New York: Harper & Row, 1962.

Mlodinow, Leonard. *The Drunkard's Walk: How Randomness Rules Our Lives*. Kindle edition. New York: Pantheon Books, 2008.

Paulos, John Allen. *Innumeracy: Mathematical Illiteracy and Its Consequences*. New York: Hill and Wang, 1988.

Plato. *Phaedrus*. Edited by Alexander Nehamas and Paul Woodruff. Indianapolis: Hackett Publishing Company, 1995.

Poundstone, William. *Prisoner's Dilemma*. Kindle edition. New York: Knopf Doubleday Publishing Group, 2011.

Public Broadcasting Service. *Nova, Making Stuff Faster*. October 16, 2013.

Shepley, James. "How Dulles Averted War: Three Times, New Disclosures Show, He Brought Us Back from the Brink." *Life*, January 1956, 70–80.

Shermer, Michael. *The Believing Brain: From Ghosts and Gods to Politics and Conspiracies—How We Construct Beliefs and Reinforce Them as Truths*. New York: Times Books, 2011.

Siegel, Eric. *Predictive Analytics: The Power to Predict Who Will Click, Buy, Lie, or Die*. Kindle edition. Hoboken, NJ: Wiley, 2013.

Steffen, Jason Hyrum. Airplanes. Accessed September 10, 2014. http://home.fnal.gov/~jsteffen/airplanes.html.

Stout, Martha, and Shelly Frasier. *The Sociopath Next Door*. Old Saybrook, CT: Tantor Media, 2005.

Swann, Maxine. "The Professor, the Bikini Model and the Suitcase Full of Trouble." *New York Times Magazine*, March 8, 2011. Accessed September 10, 2014. http://www.nytimes.com/2013/03/10/magazine/the-professor-the-bikini-model-and-the-suitcase-full-of-trouble.html?pagewanted=all&_r=0.

Taleb, Nassim Nicholas. *The Black Swan: The Impact of the Highly Improbable*. New York: Random House, 2007.

Thaler, Richard H., and Cass R. Sunstein. *Nudge: Improving Decisions about Health, Wealth, and Happiness*. New Haven, CT: Yale University Press, 2008.

Wansink, Brian. *Mindless Eating: Why We Eat More Than We Think*. Kindle edition. New York: Random House Publishing Group, 2006.

Wilson, Timothy D. *Strangers to Ourselves: Discovering the Adaptive Unconscious*. Cambridge, MA: Belknap Press, 2004.

Young, Aaron, Humayun J. Chaudhry, Jon V. Thomas, and Michael Dugan. "A Census of Actively Licensed Physicians in the United States, 2012." *Journal of Medical Regulation* 99, no. 2. Accessed September 10, 2014. http://www.fsmb.org/pdf/census.pdf.